C000163040

WALKING ON LA PALMA

About the Author

Paddy Dillon is a prolific walker and guidebook writer, with over 90 books to his name and contributions to 40 other titles. He has written for several outdoor magazines and other publications.

Paddy uses a tablet computer to write as he walks. His descriptions are therefore precise, having been written at the very point at which the reader uses them. Paddy is an indefatigable long-distance walker who has walked all of Britain's National Trails and several European trails. He has also walked in Nepal, Tibet, Korea and the Rocky Mountains of Canada and the US. Paddy is a member of the Outdoor Writers and Photographers Guild and President of the Backpackers Club.

Other Cicerone guides written by Paddy include:

Glyndwr's Way
Mountain Walking in Mallorca
The Cleveland Way and the
    Yorkshire Wolds Way
The GR5 Trail
The GR20 Corsica
The Great Glen Way
The Irish Coast to Coast Walk
The Mountains of Ireland
The National Trails
The North York Moors
The Pennine Way
The Reivers Way
The South West Coast Path
The Teesdale Way (Martin Collins;
    updated by Paddy Dillon)
The Wales Coast Path
Trekking in Greenland
Trekking in Mallorca

Trekking in the Alps (contributing
    author)
Walking and Trekking in Iceland
Walking in County Durham
Walking in Menorca
Walking in Sardinia
Walking in the Isles of Scilly
Walking in the North Pennines
Walking on Arran
Walking on Gran Canaria
Walking on Guernsey
Walking on Jersey
Walking on La Gomera and El
    Hierro
Walking on Lanzarote and
    Fuerteventura
Walking on Madeira
Walking on Malta
Walking on Tenerife

WALKING ON LA PALMA

INCLUDING THE GR130 AND GR131
LONG-DISTANCE TRAILS

by Paddy Dillon

JUNIPER HOUSE, MURLEY MOSS,
OXENHOLME ROAD, KENDAL, CUMBRIA LA9 7RL
www.cicerone.co.uk

© Paddy Dillon 2019
Second edition 2019
ISBN: 978 1 85284 853 8
First edition 2010

This book is the first in a series of five guides to walking on the Canary Islands, replacing Paddy Dillon's previous Cicerone guides:

Walking in the Canary Islands, Vol 1: West
ISBN: 978 1 85284 365 6
Walking in the Canary Islands, Vol 2: East
ISBN: 978 1 85284 368 7

Printed by KHL Printing, Singapore.

A catalogue record for this book is available from the British Library.

All photographs are by the author unless otherwise stated.

Updates to this Guide

While every effort is made by our authors to ensure the accuracy of guidebooks as they go to print, changes can occur during the lifetime of an edition. Any updates that we know of for this guide will be on the Cicerone website (www.cicerone.co.uk/853/updates), so please check before planning your trip. We also advise that you check information about such things as transport, accommodation and shops locally. Even rights of way can be altered over time. We are always grateful for information about any discrepancies between a guidebook and the facts on the ground, sent by email to updates@cicerone.co.uk or by post to Cicerone, Juniper House, Murley Moss, Oxenholme Road, Kendal LA9 7RL.

Register your book: To sign up to receive free updates, special offers and GPX files where available, register your book at www.cicerone.co.uk.

Front cover: Enjoying views across the Caldera de Taburiente from Pico de la Nieve (Walks 5, 34 and 44)

CONTENTS

Map key 7
Overview map 9

INTRODUCTION 11
Location 12
Geology 12
Wildlife 13
National parks 16
The Fortunate Isles 17
Getting there 18
When to go 19
Accommodation 19
Health and safety 20
Food and drink 20
Language 21
Money 21
Communications 22

WALKING ON LA PALMA 23
Getting there 25
Getting around 25
What to take 26
Waymarking and access 26
Maps 27
Food and drink 28
Tourist information offices 28
Emergencies 28
Using this guide 28

THE WALKS
1   Santa Cruz and Lomo de las Nieves 30
2   Fuentes de Las Breñas 35
3   Buenavista and Pico de las Ovejas 38
4   Santa Cruz and Montaña de Tagoja 42
5   Pico de la Nieve to Santa Cruz 45
6   Santa Cruz to Puerto de Tazacorte 49
7   El Paso to Refugio del Pilar 54
8   Refugio del Pilar to Santa Cruz 56
9   Refugio del Pilar to Playa del Hoyo 63
10   Refugio del Pilar to Playa del Hoyo or La Salemera 67

11	Refugio del Pilar and Pico Nambroque	72
12	Jedey to Tigalate	75
13	San Nicolás and Coladas de San Juan	79
14	Llanos del Jable and Coladas de San Juan	82

Caldera de Taburiente 85

15	Pico Bejenado	87
16	La Cumbrecita to La Cancelita and Los Llanos	90
17	Barranco de las Angustias and Caldera de Taburiente	93
18	La Cumbrecita to Caldera de Taburiente	99
19	Caldera de Taburiente and Hoya Verde	103

20	Tijarafe and Porís de Candelaria	105
21	Tinizara to Piedras Altas and Tijarafe	108
22	La Traviesa: El Time to Briesta	112
23	La Traviesa: Briesta to Barlovento	117
24	La Zarza and Don Pedro	123
25	Roque del Faro to Garafía	127
26	Roque del Faro and Franceses	130
27	Roque del Faro to Roque de los Muchachos	134
28	Roque de los Muchachos to Puntagorda or Tijarafe	138
29	Pico de la Cruz to Barlovento	142
30	Pico de la Cruz to Los Sauces or Barlovento	146
31	Los Sauces and Los Tilos	151
32	Fuente de Olén to Las Lomadas	156
33	Fuente Vizcaína to La Galga	160
34	Pico de la Nieve to Puntallana or Tenagua	165
35	GR130: Santa Cruz de La Palma to Mazo	170
36	GR130: Mazo to Fuencaliente	173
37	GR130: Fuencaliente to Los Llanos	177
38	GR130: Los Llanos to Puntagorda	183
39	GR130: Puntagorda to Garafía	189
40	GR130: Garafía to Franceses	193
41	GR130: Franceses to Los Sauces	197
42	GR130: Los Sauces to Santa Cruz de La Palma	202
43	GR131: Puerto de Tazacorte to Roque de los Muchachos	209
44	GR131: Roque de los Muchachos to Refugio del Pilar	213
45	GR131: Refugio del Pilar to Faro de Fuencaliente	218

APPENDIX A	Route summary table	224
APPENDIX B	Topographical glossary	229
APPENDIX C	Useful contacts	230

Map Key

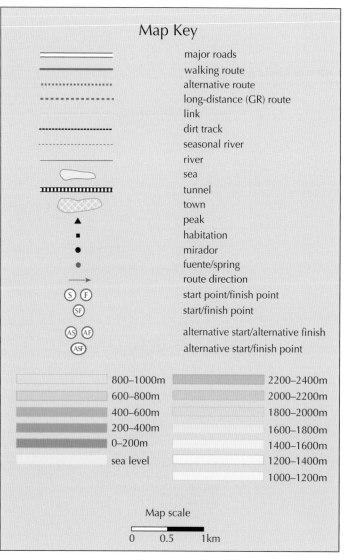

	major roads
	walking route
	alternative route
	long-distance (GR) route
	link
	dirt track
	seasonal river
	river
	sea
	tunnel
	town
▲	peak
■	habitation
●	mirador
•	fuente/spring
→	route direction
Ⓢ Ⓕ	start point/finish point
ⓈⒻ	start/finish point
ⒶⓈ ⒶⒻ	alternative start/alternative finish
ⒶⓈⒻ	alternative start/finish point

	800–1000m		2200–2400m
	600–800m		2000–2200m
	400–600m		1800–2000m
	200–400m		1600–1800m
	0–200m		1400–1600m
	sea level		1200–1400m
			1000–1200m

Map scale

0   0.5   1km

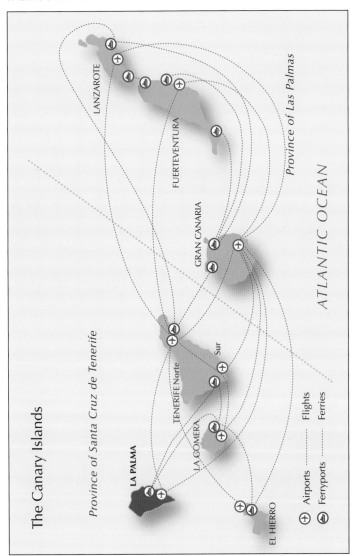

The Canary Islands

Province of Santa Cruz de Tenerife

Province of Las Palmas

ATLANTIC OCEAN

LANZAROTE

FUERTEVENTURA

GRAN CANARIA

TENERIFE Norte

Sur

LA GOMERA

LA PALMA

EL HIERRO

Airports — Flights
Ferryports — Ferries

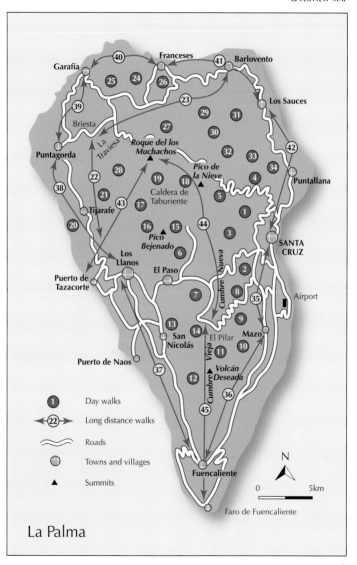

La Palma

① Day walks

◄②②► Long distance walks

〜 Roads

⬤ Towns and villages

▲ Summits

N

0 ———— 5km

A view of Pico Bejenado, seen from a vineyard high above San Nicolás (Walk 13)

INTRODUCTION

The little seaside village of La Salamera and its distinctive tall lighthouse (Walk 10)

The seven sub-tropical Canary Islands bask in sunny splendour off the Atlantic coast of north-west Africa. Millions of sun-starved north Europeans flock there for beach holidays, but increasingly visitors are discovering the amazing variety of landscapes throughout the archipelago. Conditions range from semi-deserts to perpetually moist *laurisilva* 'cloud forests', from rugged cliff coasts to high mountains, from fertile cultivation terraces to awesome rocky *barrancos* carved deep into multi-coloured layers of volcanic bedrock. Some areas are given the highest possible protection as national parks, but there are many more types of protected landscapes, rural parks, natural monuments and nature reserves.

More and more walkers are finding their feet, exploring the Canary Islands using centuries-old mule tracks, rugged cliff paths and forest trails. Paths pick their way between cultivation terraces, squeeze between houses and make their way to rugged coves and hidden beaches. Some paths run from village to village, following old mule tracks once used to transport goods, while other paths are based on pilgrim trails to and from remote churches and *ermitas*. Many have been cleared, repaired, signposted and waymarked in recent years, ready to be explored and enjoyed.

This guidebook explores the way-marked trail networks on the island of La Palma. Despite its small size, there are routes of all types – from easy strolls to hands-on scrambling, from simple day-walks to long-distance trails. As these routes are fully signposted and waymarked, walkers can follow them with confidence and enjoy the islands to the full. Almost 900km (560 miles) of trails are described in this guidebook.

LOCATION

The Canary Islands are more or less enclosed in a rectangular area from 13°30'W to 18°00'W and 27°30'N to 29°30'N. As a group, they stretch west to east over 450km (280 miles). Although administered by Spain, the mother country is 1100km (685 miles) away. The narrowest strait between the Canary Islands and Africa is a mere 110km (70 miles). The total land area is almost 7500km² (2900 square miles), but the sea they occupy is 10 times that size.

GEOLOGY

Most of the world's volcanic land-scapes are formed where huge continental or oceanic 'plates' collide with each other. When continental plates collide, the Earth's crust crumples upwards to form mountains, and when plates are torn apart, basaltic rock from deep within the Earth's mantle erupts to form mountains. The Canary Islands, however, are different, and have a complicated geological history.

The African landmass is the visible part of a continental plate that extends into the Atlantic Ocean, but the Canary Islands lie within the oceanic crust of the eastern Atlantic Ocean, close to the passive junction with the African continental plate. It is thought that the islands now lie directly above a hot-spot, or mantle plume, some 2500km (1550 miles) deep within the Earth. The mantle plume is fixed, but the oceanic and African plates are drifting very slowly eastwards. Every so often a split in the oceanic crust opens above the mantle plume, allowing molten rock to vent onto the ocean floor. As more and more material erupts, it piles higher and higher until it rises from the sea. Each of the Canary Islands was formed this way.

Lanzarote and Fuerteventura were the first Canary Islands to form, and were subsequently pulled east-wards. The next time a rift opened over the mantle plume the islands of Gran Canaria and Tenerife were formed, and these were in turn pulled eastwards. A further oceanic rift led to the formation of La Gomera, La Palma and El Hierro. Looking forward in geological time more islands will appear as other rifts are torn open in the future.

Shepherds once used long poles to negotiate steep and rocky terrain and local walkers still use them

The forces at work deep within the Earth can scarcely be imagined. Every single piece of rock throughout the Canary Islands once existed in a molten state. Consider the energy needed to melt one small stone, and multiply that to imagine the energy required to melt everything in the island chain, as well as the immense amount of rock beneath the sea that supports them all!

Over time huge amounts of volcanic material were piled high, but erosion has led to great instability. During recent geological time vast chunks of the islands have collapsed into the sea, creating features such as El Golfo on El Hierro, the Caldeira de Taburiente on La Palma, and the Orotava valley on Tenerife. With each catastrophic collapse, tidal waves devastated places around the Atlantic Ocean. Geologists predict that similar collapses could occur in the future on the Cumbre Nueva on La Palma, or the north face of El Teide on Tenerife.

WILDLIFE

Plants and flowers

While the northern hemisphere was in the grip of an Ice Age, the Canary Islands were sluiced by rainstorms, with powerful rivers carving deep, steep-sided barrancos into unstable layers of ash and lava. As the land-masses emerged from the Ice Age the Canary Islands dried out and the vegetation had to adapt to survive. Some species are well adapted to semi-desert conditions, while on the highest parts of the islands, laurisilva cloud forests are able to trap moisture from the mists and keep themselves well watered. Laurisilva forests once spread all the way round Mediterranean and tropical regions, and one of the best remnants on La Palma is found at Los Tilos.

Canary pines flourish on high, dry mountainsides, sometimes in places where nothing else grows. Almost every pine you see will have a scorched trunk, but they regenerate surprisingly well after forest fires. Beware of the long pine needles on

1 *Rock rose is often the only shrub that grows among tall Canary pines, yet flourishes in those places*

2 *'Sticky broom' covers the highest mountains on La Palma and features yellow flowers in spring*

3 *Canary pines often feature scorched trunks, but regenerate well following forest fires*

the ground, as they are slippery underfoot. Canary palms also flourish in dry places, and in the past every part of the tree had a use; today they provide delicious *miel de palma*, or palm honey. Every so often dragon trees occur, the last surviving descendants of the ancient prehistoric forests. They have been decimated in the wild but prove popular in gardens.

Tagasaste trees are often found in dense plantations, always in places where livestock are grazed. They grow with little water, yet have a high nutritional content and are regularly cut for animal fodder. In recent years they have been exported to Australia. Junipers are common; fruit and nut trees have been established, including apples, oranges, lemons, bananas, almonds, figs and vines. The introduced prickly pears are abundant, not so much for their fruit, but for raising cochineal beetles, whose blood provides a vivid red dye.

14

Bushy scrub is rich and varied, including sticky-leaved cistus and a host of species that walkers should learn to identify. These include bushy, rubbery *tabaibal* and the tall *cardón*, or candelabra spurge. Both have milky latex sap, as does tangled *cornical*, with its distinctive horned seed pods, which creeps over the ground and drystone walls. *Aulaga* looks like a tangled mass of spines and is often found colonising old cultivation terraces in arid areas. Aromatic, pale green *incienso* is a bushy plant that, with *salado*, grows densely on the arid lower slopes of the islands. The fragrant Canarian lavender usually grows in arid, rocky, stony areas among other scrub species. Few of the plants have common English names, but all of them feature so often that they should be learned.

Flowers grow all year round, but visitors in spring and early summer will be amazed at the colour and wealth of flowering plants. Many are Canarian endemics, and even trying to compile a shortlist would be pointless. Anyone with a particular interest in flowers and other plants should carry a specific field guide, in English. Try *Native Flora of the Canary Islands* by Miguel Ángel Cabrera Pérez, (Editorial Everest) or *Wild Flowers of the Canary Islands* by David Bramwell and Zoë Bramwell, (Editorial Rueda).

Animals
As befits remote islands created in relatively recent geological time, the main animal groups to colonise the land were winged creatures, insects and birds. The largest indigenous land mammals were bats. Large and small

The largest lizards on La Palma feature startlingly blue and baggy throats

Herds of goats are often encountered while walking. Their milk is used to make cheese

a flash of colour. The islands attract plenty of passage migrants, as well as escapees from aviaries. The coastal fringes are colonised by gulls, but it is best to take a boat trip to spot shearwaters or storm petrels, as they spend most of their time on open water. Boat trips are also the way to spot a variety of dolphins and whales.

Once the Guanche people arrived and colonised the islands over 2000 years ago, the forests suffered as much from clearance as from grazing by voracious sheep and goats. Following the Conquest in the 15th century, the Spaniards brought other domestic animals; of these the cats had a particularly devastating impact on the native wildlife, practically wiping out giant Canarian lizards, which have only recently been rescued from the edge of extinction. The largest lizards on La Palma are noted for their startlingly blue throats. Rabbits chew their way through the vegetation and appear regularly on Canarian menus.

lizards also arrived, possibly clinging to driftwood. The laurisilva cloud forest is home to the laurel pigeon, while the rock pigeon prefers cliffs. Buzzards and kestrels can be spotted hunting, while ospreys are struggling. Ravens and choughs are common in some places. There are several varieties of pipits, chaffinches, warblers and chiffchaffs. One of the smallest birds is the kinglet, a relative of the goldcrest. There are canaries, which have nothing to do with the name of the islands, and parakeets that add

NATIONAL PARKS

The Canary Islands contain a handful of national parks and many other protected areas. Parque Nacional de Taburiente is in the middle of La Palma, extending to the highest peaks. The whole island has been designated as a World Biosphere Reserve. Other protected areas on the island include Parque Rural (Rural Park), Parque Natural (Natural Park), Paisaje Protegido (Protected Land),

Reserva Natural Especial (Special Nature Reserve), Monumento Natural (Natural Monument), and so on. Prominent notices usually tell walkers when they are entering or leaving these areas. Very little territory lies outside one of these places! There are visitor centres where more information can be studied, and where interesting literature is on sale.

THE FORTUNATE ISLES

Myths and legends speak of 'The Fortunate Isles', or 'Isles of the Blessed', lying somewhere in the Atlantic, enjoying a wonderful climate and bearing all manner of fruit. The rebel Roman general Sertorius planned to retire there, while Plutarch referred to them many times, although Pliny warned 'these islands, however, are greatly annoyed by the putrefying bodies of monsters, which are constantly thrown up by the sea'. Maybe these scribes knew of the Canary Islands, or maybe they were drawing on older Phoenician or Carthaginian references. Some would even claim that the islands were the last remnants of Atlantis.

The Gaunches, often described as a 'stone-age' civilisation, settled on the Canary Islands well over 2000 years ago, and Cro-Magnon Man was there as early as 3000BC. No-one knows where the Guanches came from, but it seems likely that they arrived from North Africa in fleets of canoes. Although technologically primitive, their society was well ordered, and they had a special regard for monumental rock-forms in the mountains.

A level area of ash is flanked by pines at Llano de los Guanches

The Guanches fiercely resisted the well-armed Spaniards during the 15th century Conquest of the islands, but one by one each island fell. Tenerife capitulated last of all, with the mighty volcano of El Teide grumbling throughout. Many Guanches were slaughtered or enslaved, but some entered into treaties, converted to Christianity and inter-married. They lost their land and freedom, but their blood flows in the veins of native Canarios.

The Canary Islands were visited by Christopher Columbus on his voyage of discovery in 1492. Subsequently they were used as stepping stones to the Americas, and many Canarios emigrated. The islands were exposed and not always defended with military might; they were subject to pirate raids, endured disputes with the Portuguese, were attacked by the British and suffered wavering economic fortunes.

There was constant rivalry between Tenerife and Gran Canaria, with the entire island group being governed from Las Palmas de Gran Canaria from 1808, before Santa Cruz de Tenerife became the capital in 1822. In 1927 the Canary Islands were divided into two provinces – Las Palmas and Santa Cruz de Tenerife.

In the early 20th century the military governor of the Canary Islands, General Franco, departed for North Africa to launch a military coup. This marked the onset of the infamous Civil War, leading to the creation of the Spanish Republic, and was followed by a long repressive dictatorship. The Canary Islands remained free of the worst strife of the Civil War, but also became something of a backwater. It was largely as a result of Franco's later policies that the Canary Islands were developed in the 1960s as a major destination for northern Europeans.

Since 1982 the islands have been an autonomous region and there have been calls for complete independence from Spain. The islanders regard themselves as 'Canarios' first and 'Spanish' second, although they are also fiercely loyal to their own particular islands, towns and villages.

GETTING THERE

There are occasional direct flights from the UK to La Palma, and the island is also served from Tenerife. There are plenty of options for flying to Tenerife, scheduled or charter, from a range of British and European airports. The hardest part is checking all the 'deals' to find an airport, operator, schedules and prices that suit. Most international flights land at Tenerife Sur, but inter-island flights operate from Tenerife Norte. Transferring between airports can be expensive and time-consuming, and it may be easier to catch the next ferry.

Frequent, fast and cheap TITSA buses link Tenerife Sur with Los Cristianos, and the taxi fare is reasonable. If a night's accommodation is needed at Los Cristianos, there are abundant options around the resort. The bus stops, main hotels and ferryport are all within easy walking distance of each other. Two ferry companies operate to La Palma: Lineas Fred Olsen and Naviera Armas.

WHEN TO GO

Most people visit the Canary Islands in summer, but it is usually too hot for walking. Winter weather is often good, but on La Palma expect some cloud cover and rain on the midslopes and possibly snow on the highest parts. Spring weather is sunny and clear; the vegetation is fresh and features an amazing wealth of flowers. Autumn weather is often good, but the vegetation often seems rather scorched after the summer.

ACCOMMODATION

Most visitors to the Canary Islands opt for a package deal, so they are tied to a single accommodation base in a faceless resort. This is far from ideal and a base in the 'wrong' place can make it difficult to get to and from walking routes. Package deals are seldom available on the island of La Palma; however, out of season, walkers would have little problem turning up unannounced at hotels or pensións, or booking at the last minute on accommodation websites such as www.airbnb.com or www.booking.com. A network of hostels (*albergues*) has been established for the use of walkers, and details can be obtained from the website www.senderosdelapalma.es. Opportunities to camp are very limited, and camping in the Caldera de Taburiente requires a permit from the national park authorities. Wild camping is technically illegal, but it does take place. **Note** La Palma does not have mountain refuges in the way that European walkers might expect.

Wayside crosses are often decorated on 3 May to celebrate the discovery of the True Cross in AD325

19

Most of the routes are accessible using buses, but be sure to carry up-to-date timetables if using them

couldn't contract at home. Water on La Palma is either drawn from rainfall, or generated by the laurisilva cloud forests. It soaks into the ground, is filtered through thick beds of volcanic ash and emerges pure and clean, perfectly safe to drink. Bottled water is available if you prefer, but buy it cheaply from supermarkets rather than at considerable expense from bars. There are no snakes, no stinging insects worse than honey-bees, and there are always warning signs near hives. Don't annoy dogs and they won't annoy you. Dogs that are likely to bite are nearly always tethered, so keep away.

In case of a medical emergency, dial 112 for an ambulance. In case of a non-emergency, all islands have hospitals, health centres (*Centro de Salud*) and chemists (*Farmacia*). If treatment is required, EU citizens should present their European Health Insurance Card, while British citizens should check arrangements following Brexit.

Refugio del Pilar is a recreation area with a campsite, not a mountain refuge and Refugio Punto de los Roques is a bare, unstaffed hut without running water.

HEALTH AND SAFETY

There are no nasty diseases on the Canary Islands, or, at least, nothing you

FOOD AND DRINK

Every town and most of the villages throughout the Canary Islands have bars. Most bars also double as cafés or restaurants, often serving tapas, which are often in glass cabinets, so you can point to the ones you want to eat. There are also shops selling local and imported foodstuffs. Always make the effort to sample local fare, which is often interesting and very tasty. The availability of refreshments is mentioned on every walking trail, but bear

Banana cultivation is important around the cliff coast of La Palma, but requires plenty of water

most resorts and large hotels there are English and German speakers. Those who travel to remote rural parts will need at least a few basic phrases of Spanish. Anyone with any proficiency in Spanish will quickly realise that the Canarios have their own accent and colloquialisms. For instance, the letter 's' often vanishes from the middle or end of words, to be replaced by a gentle 'h', or even a completely soundless gap. *'Los Cristianos'*, for example, becomes *'Loh Cri-tiano'*. A bus is referred to as an *autobus* in Spain, but as a *guagua* throughout the Canary Islands. Some natives may seize the opportunity to practise their English with you, while others may be puzzled by your command of Spanish. No matter how bad you think you sound, you will not be the worst they've heard!

in mind that opening hours are variable. Some shops take a very long lunch break, and not all businesses are open every day of the week. Some shops are closed all weekend, or at least half of Saturday and all of Sunday.

LANGUAGE

Castilian Spanish is spoken throughout the Canary Islands, although in

MONEY

The Euro is the currency of the Canary Islands. Large denomination Euro notes are difficult to use for small purchases, so avoid the €500 and €200 notes altogether, and avoid the €100 notes if you can. The rest are fine: €50, €20, €10 and €5. Coins come in €2 and €1. Small denomination coins come in values of 50c, 20c, 10c, 5c, 2c and 1c. Banks and ATMs are mentioned where they occur, if cash is

A small visitor centre at a campsite in the heart of the Caldera de Taburiente National Park

needed. Many accommodation providers accept major credit and debit cards, as will large supermarkets, but small bars, shops and cafés deal only in cash.

COMMUNICATIONS

All the towns and some of the villages have post offices (*Correos*) and public telephones. Opening times for large post offices are usually 0830–1430 Monday to Friday, 0930–1300 Saturday, closed on Sunday. Small post offices have more limited opening times. Mobile phone coverage is usually good in towns and villages, but can be completely absent elsewhere, depending on the nature of the terrain. High mountains and deep barrancos block signals. Internet access is usually offered by accommodation providers but, if relying on it, please check when making a booking.

WALKING ON
LA PALMA

The mouth of the Barranco del Jurado, with the zigzag path used on the ascent on the other side (Walk 20)

WALKING ON LA PALMA

Enjoying views of Caldera de Taburiente and Pico Bejenado from Mirador de Hoya Garande (Walk 43)

La Palma is one of the smaller Canary Islands, at the western end of the archipelago. Its northern parts are heavily eroded, scored by dozens of steep-sided rocky barrancos. As a result, walks that lead in and out of them are often very rugged, but that shouldn't suggest that the walking is going to be too difficult for 'ordinary' walkers. In fact, almost all the routes in this guidebook follow waymarked trails, made up of narrow paths and broad tracks that often zigzag to ease the gradient.

Access to the coast is often limited to the mouths of the barrancos, as there are sheer cliffs elsewhere. By contrast, the highest parts of the island, although very rocky, have much gentler slopes. Pine forests completely

encircle the mountains, while some moist northern parts feature laurisilva 'cloud forest'. Barrancos are not as well developed further south, although the landscape has been augmented throughout recorded history by extra volcanic peaks, the latest dating only from 1971. There are extensive slopes of volcanic ash and lava, along with well-defined cones.

It takes time to explore La Palma, reputed to be one of the steepest islands on the planet, and this guidebook contains a month's walking. The main settlement of Santa Cruz is located near the sea, but others are further inland. There is no coastal road because dozens of steep-sided, rocky barrancos would have to be negotiated, and in the past it was often easier to trek over the mountains to get from one place to another. These days, walkers can enjoy trekking in and out of these canyon-like barrancos, crossing the high ridges between.

There are 45 days of walking on La Palma presented in this guide, made up of 34 one-day walks, sign-posted as PR (*pequeño recorrido*) routes, and another 11 days sign-posted as GR (*gran recorrido*) routes, which can be linked together as long-distance walks. Bear in mind that many of these routes have been followed for centuries by farmers, travellers and mules, so they should pose no problem to walkers, and they offer the best means of exploring all parts of the island. Few of these routes stand in isolation, and most of them link with one, two or more adjacent routes, so there are options to alter and adapt them, and some routes feature significant variants and extensions. A tremendously useful website is www.senderosdelapalma.es.

GETTING THERE

By air

Flights from Tenerife Norte to La Palma are operated by Binter Canarias, tel 902 391 392, www.bintercanarias.com, or Canaryfly, tel 902 808 065, www.canaryfly.es. There are no flights from Tenerife Sur. Buses meet incoming flights, offering a link to Santa Cruz de La Palma. Taxis are also available at the airport.

By ferry

Two ferry companies operate between Los Cristianos on Tenerife and Santa Cruz de La Palma. Lineas Fred Olsen, tel 902 100 107, www.fredolsen.es, is quick but expensive. Naviera Armas, tel 902 456 500, www.navieraarmas.com, is slower and cheaper. Ferries berth almost in the centre of Santa Cruz, within walking distance of all facilities and the bus stops. Both ferry companies also sail between La Palma and La Gomera, but not every day, so bear this in mind when making plans.

GETTING AROUND

By bus

La Palma has a good network of bus services operated by Transportes Insular La Palma, tel 922 411 924 or 922 414 411, www.transporteslapalma.com. Obtain an up-to-date timetable for the whole island as soon as possible, from their website, bus station at Los Llanos or tourist information offices. Tickets are for single journeys and fares are paid on boarding the bus. For the best deal, obtain a pre-paid *bono* ticket and use the on-board machine. The *bono* will be debited less than what you would pay for a ticket on board. Buses are referred to as *guaguas*, although bus stops, or *paradas*, may be marked as 'bus'.

By taxi

Long taxi rides are expensive, but short journeys are worth considering.

Taxi ranks are located in all the towns and some of the villages. Fares are fixed by the municipalities and can be inspected on demand, although negotiation might be possible.

Car hire
Some people will automatically pick up a hire car on La Palma, and this is easily arranged in advance or on arrival. In some instances, a car is useful to reach a walk in a remote location, and a car (or taxi) is essential to reach some of the walks in the high mountains. However, many of the best walks on La Palma are linear, and if you park a car at one end it can be very difficult to return to it.

Planning your Transport
To make the most of walking opportunities, and limit long and awkward travelling, it is best to choose two or three accommodation bases with good bus connections. Linear routes described in this book always start at the 'awkward' end, usually high in the mountains, to which you would need to take a taxi, and finish where you can catch a bus. The introduction to each walk has a note about the availability of public transport. If no bus is mentioned serving the start or finish, then the use of a taxi or car is implied.

WHAT TO TAKE

If planning to use one or two bases to explore, then a simple day pack is all you need, containing items you would normally take for a day's walk. Waterproofs can be lightweight and might not even be used. Footwear is a personal preference, but wear what you would normally wear for steep, rocky, stony slopes, remembering that hot feet are more likely to be a problem than wet feet. Lightweight, light-coloured clothing is best in bright sunshine, along with a sun hat and frequent applications of sunscreen. If planning to backpack around the islands, bear in mind that wild camping is technically illegal, although surprisingly popular. Lightweight kit should be carried, as a heavy pack is a cruel burden on steep slopes in hot weather. **Note** Water can be difficult to find, so try and anticipate your needs and carry enough to last until you reach a village, houses or bar where you can obtain a refill. (All such places are indicated in the text.)

WAYMARKING AND ACCESS

La Palma was the first of the Canary Islands to adopt a system for signposting and waymarking routes using standard European codes. The island has a network of short PR (*pequeño recorrido*) routes, which are marked with yellow and white paint flashes, and numbered to keep them separate. Signposts will read PR LP, with a number following the letters. These codes are quoted in the route descriptions so that walkers will always be able to check they are going the right way. There are also

GR (*gran recorrido*) routes, which are intended as long-distance walks, but can also serve as simple one-day linear walks. Some short links are marked as SL (*sendero local*), literally local walks.

Apart from signposts, routes are marked by occasional paint marks, parallel yellow and white stripes for the PR routes, with red and white stripes for the GR routes, and green and white stripes for the SL routes. These confirm that walkers are still on course, and usually appear at junctions. Left and right turns are indicated with right-angled flashes, but if the paint marks form an 'X', this indicates that a wrong turn has been made.

La Palma boasts a splendid network of signposted and waymarked trails

MAPS

The best map of La Palma is the two-sheet 1:25,000 scale La Palma Norte and La Palma Sur, published by Editorial Alpina, www.editorialalpina. com. The maps show all the way-marked trails in excellent detail. The next best map is published by the Cabildo Insular (island council), the 1:40,000 La Palma Hiking Map.

The Instituto Geográfico Nacional (IGN), www.cnig.es, publishes maps of the Canary Islands at scales of 1:50,000 and 1:25,000. These are part of the Mapa Topográfico Nacional (MTN) series. To avoid disappointment, please check the style and quality of these maps before making a purchase, since they don't show the sort of details that walkers require.

GR AND PR WAYMARKING SIGNS

	GR	PR
Correct direction		
Turn left		
Turn right		
Wrong way		

Maps can be ordered in advance from British suppliers such as: Stanfords (12–14 Long Acre, London, WC2E 9BR, tel 0207 8361321, www.stanfords.co.uk), The Map Shop (15 High Street, Upton-upon-Severn, WR8 0HJ, tel 01684 593146, www.themapshop.co.uk) or Cordee (www.cordee.co.uk).

Route maps included in this book are all at roughly 1:50,000 scale and all maps are aligned with north at the top of the page.

FOOD AND DRINK

La Palma is self-sufficient in terms of fruit, vegetables and fish. While some restaurants are cosmopolitan, others offer good local fare. Specialities include goat's cheese. Wrinkly potatoes (*papas arrugadas*) cooked in salt are surprisingly refreshing in hot weather, served with hot *mojo roja* sauce and gentler *mojo verde*.

The most popular fish dishes are based on *vieja*. If any dishes such as soups or stews need thickening, reach for the roasted flour *gofio*, which also serves as a breakfast cereal. Local wines are also available. Never pass up an opportunity to indulge in local fare!

TOURIST INFORMATION OFFICES

- Santa Cruz, tel 922 412 106
- Los Llanos, tel 922 490 072
- Mazo, tel 922 967 044

- El Paso, tel 922 485 733
- Brena Baja, tel 922 181 354
- Tazacorte, tel 922 480 803
- Fuencaliente, tel 615 390 616

EMERGENCIES

The pan-European emergency telephone number 112 is used to call for assistance throughout the Canary Islands, linking with the police, fire or ambulance service, for a response on land or at sea. The Guardia Civil telephone number is 062, and it is likely they would be involved in a response involving mountain rescue, as they generally patrol rural areas.

USING THIS GUIDE

The walks in this guide run in sequence roughly clockwise around the island from just north-west of Santa Cruz and links between routes are often possible. In total, 45 day walks are described, ranging from 7km (4½ miles) to 32km (20 miles) in length, and covering a wide variety of terrain. For each route the distance, estimated walking time, total ascent, total descent and terrain are summarised at the start, along with a note about public transport options and refreshments available. There is also a route summary table in Appendix A to help you select the best route for your location, tastes and ability.

These are all excellent stand alone routes, some circular and some requiring buses, lifts or taxis to join

Looking towards the barren, rocky summit of Roque Chico in evening light (Walk 43)

them or leave them, but some are also stages of long-distance routes. For instance, Walks 22 and 23 make use of La Traviesa, an ancient route crossing the north-west corner of the island by traversing the mid-slopes of the mountains.

Two GR routes are also covered by the last 11 walks of the guide. The circular GR130 trail takes about a week to complete and can be started and finished at any point around the island. It is very well served by buses, so it can be split at several points, quite apart from the daily stages recommended in this guidebook. Naturally, having a base in Santa Cruz and/or Los Llanos allows all the early and late buses to be used. If not using buses, then all the recommended daily stages finish with

access to accommodation, although provision will vary widely. Walks 35 to 42 describe this route clockwise from Santa Cruz in eight stages. The GR131 trail is exclusively high-level and mountainous, requiring careful planning. It is very tough with exceptionally limited facilities. Walks 43 to 45 describe this route from Puerto de Tazacorte to Fuencaliente in three stages.

On arrival on La Palma, visit the tourist information office as soon as possible. Ask for an up-to-date bus timetable, and as much information about walking opportunities as they can provide. Remember to pick up leaflets about local attractions, as they usually give full contact details, opening times and admission charges.

WALK 1

Santa Cruz and Lomo de las Nieves

Distance	8, 11 or 19km (5, 7 or 12 miles)
Start/Finish	Santa Cruz or Santuario de las Nieves
Total Ascent/Descent	410, 1180 or 1590m (1345, 3870 or 5215ft)
Time	2hr 30min, 4hr or 6hr 30min
Terrain	Roads, tracks and paths at lower levels. Narrow forest paths and rocky tunnels at a higher level. Some stretches unsuitable for vertigo sufferers.
Refreshment	Plenty of choice in Santa Cruz. Bar at Las Nieves.
Transport	Buses run regularly between Santa Cruz and Santuario de las Nieves.

This figure-of-eight route naturally offers a choice between a short circuit from Santa Cruz to Santuario de las Nieves and back, a longer walk from the Santuario, up the Barranco de la Madera, through tunnels and back downhill, or an even longer walk that uses both options.

Route includes PR LP 2.2 and PR LP 2.3

Start at the **Barco** (ship) on Avenida de las Nieves in Santa Cruz. Walk straight up the road and bear left up steps. Turn left at the top then right as marked up Calle A Rodríguez López. Turn left at a crossroads along Calle Tabaiba then climb steps as marked, past a tangled mass of mixed scrub. Turn right up a road then quickly right up more steps. Climb a road, turn left along Calle Olén, then right up a narrow path signposted PR LP 2.2.

A level path, based on an old water channel, crosses a steep and scrubby slope overlooking the town centre. It is fenced as it crosses cliffs, looking down into a barranco full of high-rise buildings. Step down to a path junction and turn right uphill for the PR LP 2.2. Climb between old **sugar mills** piled on top of each other. After zigzagging up past them, follow the path further up the old water channel along a scrub-covered ridge, passing a tangled mass of pipes.

Climb a concrete road past a few houses, curving right to reach a junction. Turn left up a concrete road and walk straight ahead to a tarmac road bend. Walk straight up the road and quickly exit left up another concrete road, joining the road at a higher level. Turn right and left to follow a road up past the Restaurante Los Almendros. Walk round a bend and turn right along a path signposted PR LP 2.2. This is stone-paved but vegetated, steepening to become stone steps below a cliff. Reach the **Molino del Remanente** beside a complex road junction and tunnel. Walk towards the tunnel and turn right down a steep bit of road underneath the main road. Turn left to walk parallel to the main road up to a church and tree-shaded plaza at **Santuario de las Nieves**. ▶

See below for a short route back to town.

For the longer route, walk behind the church and down steps between it and a bar restaurant. Walk down a road and cross the main road near a tunnel mouth. A narrow road climbs from a car park into **Barranco de la Madera**. A concrete path and track climbs past bananas then turn left up a stony track. Stay on it and avoid turnings, climbing higher into forest, often with a pipeline alongside. Pass beneath a very high pylon line, walk beside an overhanging cliff and enter the Parque Natural Las Nieves.

There is no mistaking the way ahead, past patchy laurisilva among pines and scrub, and another overhanging cliff. At a higher level the track makes a sweeping zigzag and ends at a building. Keep climbing beside a pipe or water channel in dense laurisilva. Walk along a rocky ledge beneath another overhanging cliff, unsuitable for vertigo sufferers. Climb again and go through a hole in a rocky buttress. Climb past a tunnel mouth and the path crosses the barranco and climbs a densely forested slope. Cross a scrubby slope and drop, then climb again and cross the barranco between sheer rock walls, around 1000m (3280ft).

Enter a **tunnel** to follow a water channel. A torch is useful, but isn't essential as there are lots of rock 'windows'. A narrow, fenced path leads to another tunnel, which is longer and has more windows. Another narrow, fenced path leads to another tunnel with windows. The next stretch out in the open is quite long, then there is a little rock arch, followed by another long stretch of path. The last tunnel is fairly short, but watch for boulders inside.

Following a water channel through a tunnel, peeping through a 'window' into the Barranco de la Madera

The path emerges and leads to a water regulator, then drops and zigzags steeply on a forested slope. First it overlooks Barranco de la Madera, then **Barranco del Río**, as it switches side to side down the Lomo de las Nieves. Pine forest has a laurisilva understorey, giving way to cistus and rock rose further down. Pass a pylon and leave the forest to pass a little house beside big eucalyptus trees. Cross a concrete track and go down a path veering away from it, leading back down to the Santuario de las Nieves. ▶

The short walk continues from here.

Just across the road from the church, a cobbled path is signposted as the PR LP 2.2 Ruta de los Molinos. This was followed earlier, parallel to the main road, so follow it back to where a bit of road runs beneath the main road. Turn left as signposted for Santa Cruz, following a track down the **Barranco de las Nieves**. Cross the barranco again and again as marked and signposted, past a smelly farm. A patchy road crosses later and is followed to a main road. Turn left down the main road towards a tunnel then left down a slip road as marked, under the main road and tunnel mouth. Simply walk straight down Calle Leocricia Pestana, down Avenida M Gonzalez Mendez, turning right to cross a bridge over the barranco, then left down the other side. Pass a wider bridge to return to the Barco in **Santa Cruz**.

WALK 2

Fuentes de Las Breñas

Distance	10km (6¼ miles)
Start/Finish	Breña Alta
Total Ascent/Descent	550m (1805ft)
Time	2hr 45min
Terrain	Roads and tracks at lower levels. Steep, rugged, winding forest paths at higher levels.
Refreshment	Plenty of choice in Breña Alta. Bar at El Llanito.
Transport	Buses serve Breña Alta from Santa Cruz and Los Llanos.

This interesting circuit climbs forested slopes above Breña Alta, visiting a series of old water sources, or *fuentes*. People used to obtain fresh water from them, which is now piped to their properties. In its lower parts, the route passes 17th-century gateways onto old estates.

Route uses PR LP 19, PR LP 18.2 and GR130.

Start at the church of San Pedro in **Breña Alta**, around 360m (1180ft). Cross to the police station and go to the far end of a car park, leaving it by road. Turn right up steps to reach another road and turn left to leave town. Cross a bridge over **Barranco de Aguasencio** and turn right as signposted for Fuentes de Las Breñas. Climb the concrete road and avoid all turnings to properties, continuing straight up a tarmac road with fruit to the right, scrub on the left and laurisilva forest rising higher.

35

A series of inter-connected water troughs at Fuente Chavez high above Breña Alta

When the road forks at a huddle of buildings, keep left and pass under a concrete arch. The road ends and a path climbs the bed of the barranco, passing **Fuente Chavez** and its *lavadero* (communal washing place). The path climbs steps into dense laurisilva, with rock walls above. Cross the bed of the barranco and swing left up to a junction. A detour down to the left leads to **Fuente Nueva**, otherwise keep climbing the steep, rocky, wooded slope.

Pass a signpost and the path undulates around 600m (1970ft) among chestnuts before heading downhill. Steep log steps drop to a footbridge, then stone steps lead to **Fuente Espinel** at the base of a cliff. Climb stone steps and cross a felled slope. Cross a rutted track and walk down a slope to cross another track, continuing down into a wooded valley. Climb again, cross a road and walk down a track as marked and signposted, down a path into woods. A three-way signpost indicates a short detour up to **Fuente Melchora**, before the route heads down to the rocky bed of a valley.

Climb from the woods and descend past a pylon into a partly wooded valley. Climb from it and turn left down a track, right down another track, into a valley of laurisilva and chestnut. Climb again and turn left down another track, into a rock-walled barranco in laurisilva, where there is another three-way signpost. A detour up the brambly bed reveals steps climbing to **Fuente Aduares**. Double back and the route later climbs steep stone steps on a well-wooded slope. Turn left as marked down to a track then turn left down the track into a valley of mixed woodland.

Eventually, a signpost and yellow/white flash mark a right turn up a rugged, wooded path. This passes a shrine at the base of a cliff, turning left to climb above it. Turn right along a track, gently down and up around a valley. Turn left down a road and climb to another three-way signpost on a road bend at **La Sociedad**, around 500m (1640ft).

At this point, the PR LP 18.2 (Walk 8) descends from Refugio del Pilar. Turn left straight down Camino La Piedad and down past Cruz de La Piedad. Pass a road bend and go down a narrow concrete road with some old stone paving. Turn left down a tarmac road as signposted, past Cruz de La Unión and a 17th-century gateway. The Camino La Unión leads to a junction with a main road at **El Llanito**. ▶

Turn right for a bus stop and bar.

Turn left to cross a bridge over Barranco de Aduares and veer right down Camino las Curias. Pass a small tile furnace and continue along the road, past another 17th-century gateway. Walk down and up concrete and tarmac, to the end of the road. Make quick left and right turns as marked, then climb a short, steep, narrow, winding concrete road to Cruz de la Dura. Turn left up the concrete road back into Breña Alta (banks with ATMs, post office, shops, bars, restaurants, buses and taxis).

WALK 3

Buenavista and Pico de las Ovejas

Distance	13km (8 miles)
Start	Restaurante La Graja, Buenavista
Finish	Restaurante Los Almendros, Velhoco
Total Ascent	1550m (5085ft)
Total Descent	1590m (5215ft)
Time	5hr
Terrain	Easy tracks at the start and finish, otherwise very steep forest paths.
Refreshment	Bars at Buenavista and Velhoco.
Transport	Buses serve Buenavista and Velhoco from Santa Cruz.
Note	Approach this route with caution, as half of the route has been listed as 'closed' for some time.

There are two paths on the exceptionally steep forested slope between Santa Cruz and Pico de las Ovejas. It's important to use the PR LP 2.1 for the ascent, and the PR LP 2 for the descent, as both are awkward if reversed. Around 350m (1150ft) of ascent/descent from Santa Cruz can be saved using buses.

Route uses PR LP 2.1 and PR LP 2.

If walking all the way from Santa Cruz, start by following Walk 35 from the town centre to the Restaurante La Graja at **Buenavista**, then walk up Camino La Estrella. Huge walls guard oranges and date palms, while the Monasterio del Císter lies to the right. Further uphill, the PR LP 2.1 is signposted for Pico de las Ovejas along the Camino la Corsillada. Worryingly, it bears the words 'sendero muy peligroso' (very dangerous path).

Follow the concrete track down to the bed of **Barranco de Juan Mayor** and keep straight ahead up a stony track beneath a concrete bridge. Pass a house and follow the track up through the barranco, passing small buildings. Keep low among mixed laurisilva, pine and chestnuts, eventually reaching a water pump building

between two forested barrancos. Turn right up stone steps and continue up a steep earth path in dense laurisilva. Cross a concrete water channel then climb log steps on the forested slope. The path is clear, but relentlessly steep.

When a slight dip is reached on the forested crest, next to a rocky, forested hump, the altitude is close to 1100m (3610ft). Climb a dark, bouldery groove, with more light reaching the ground later, where more plants grow. Pass big pines among

The Monasterio del Císter occupies the only area of flat ground and is passed at the start of the walk

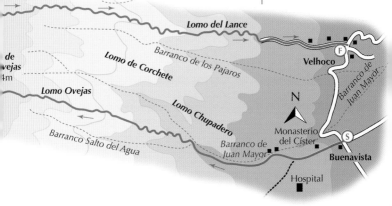

Path junction on the crest near the summit of Pico de las Ovejas

the laurisilva on **Lomo Ovejas**, then laurisilva gives way to pines, heather and rock rose. The gradient eases a little and there are some log steps on the approach to a high crest, where the GR131 is joined (see Walk 44).

Turn right to follow a path flanked by parallel lines of stones. It climbs and passes close to **Pico de las Ovejas**, whose 1854m (6082ft) summit is just to the left. Continue along the gently undulating path, crossing a gap then climbing. As the pines become dense, watch for a path down to the right at **La Tabladita**. This is flanked by parallel lines of stones and is flashed yellow/white as the PR LP 2.

Take care not to slip on stones, pine needles and pine cones.

Descend steeply past pines and rock rose along a ridge. ◄ The forest becomes dense, with pine and laurisilva. There is a slight rise, around 1250m (4100ft), past three big pines on the crest. Head steeply down through dense laurisilva, following a deep groove, passing a rock wall, briefly levelling out among pines. This is **Lomo del Lance**, around 1000m (3280ft). Go down another steep groove, noticing chestnuts, then zigzag down a steep slope of pines. Follow a wall down a slope of chestnuts to reach a concrete road.

Pass barking dogs and walk down the steep road, past oranges, avocados and houses at Barranquero de San Vicente. Reach a road at a prominent wayside cross. Turn left to reach a bus shelter at **Velhoco**, or walk further down the road to reach the Restaurante Los Almendros. It is possible to continue down to Santa Cruz by referring to Walk 1.

The route follows a well-trodden path near Pico de las Ovejas

WALK 4
Santa Cruz and Montaña de Tagoja

Distance	15km (9½ miles)
Start/Finish	Barco, Santa Cruz
Total Ascent/Descent	1150m (3770ft)
Time	5hr
Terrain	Steep roads, tracks and paths, climbing urban, cultivated and forested slopes, then descending steeply.
Refreshment	Plenty of choice in Santa Cruz. Bar at Candelaria.
Transport	Buses serve Mirca and Candelaria from Santa Cruz.

Montaña de Tagoja rises impressively above Santa Cruz, but is a mere foothill far removed from the main mountain crest of La Palma. A very bendy road climbs past it, while a path makes a direct ascent. This is easily linked with another path to descend, and the route can be shortened by bus.

Route uses GR130, PR LP 3.1 and PR LP 3.

Leave the Barco (ship) in **Santa Cruz** and follow the nearby coastal Avenida Marítima across a river to a map-board. Follow the coast road signposted for Puntallana, past the Apartamentos Rocamar. Don't walk up the main road, but follow the road running level past buildings, through a small industrial site. Turn left up a track flanked by calcosas, tabaibal and verode, reaching the bed of the **Barranco de El Dorador**. Turn left up it, then turn right to follow a path zigzagging up to the main road at a map-board.

Turn right up the road, left at a roundabout, using a pedestrian crossing in front of a tunnel. Climb a narrow tarmac and concrete road flashed red/white and keep straight ahead at a junction of concrete roads. Climb straight up a short, steep tarmac road, signposted PR LP 3.1 for Pico de la Nieve. Climb steps and another steep concrete road. Follow yellow/white flashes to reach a complex road junction and bus shelter at **La Verada**. Climb a steep concrete road to short-cut a bend from the main road, then turn left up the main road at **Mirca**.

Turn left up another concrete road and as it becomes excessively steep, turn right along a narrow, scrubby, overgrown path. Follow this to the main road and turn right to pass the 17th-century church of **Nuestra Señora de Candelaria** and a bar, at almost 300m (985ft). ▶ A nearby road is signposted for Roque de los Muchachos, but is far too bendy to walk. Instead, walk down the main road to find signposts on a bend. Follow a road uphill then turn left up a steep concrete and stone-paved path to a road at **Los Alamos**.

Use buses to start here.

Cross the road and climb straight up a concrete road. Turn left as marked, then immediately right up a steep, grassy path. The path climbs very direct and clips four bends on the mountain road, with pines on the higher slopes. Keep climbing and cross a couple of tracks, then follow part of a track, but watch for the path marked up a winding groove on a slope of pines and stunted laurisilva. Emerge at a junction of tracks and walk straight ahead along the middle one. Pass a cultivated hollow and later watch for a path marked up to the left. This winds up a groove on the forested slope, reaching the mountain road again.

Barranco Barbuzano

▲1089m
Montaña
de Tagoja

Asomada Alta

N

Los
Alamos

Nuestra Señora
de Candelaria

Mirca

El Dorador

La
Verada

Barranco de El Dorador

Tunnels

La Palmita

SANTA
CRUZ

SF Barco

Looking down towards Santa Cruz from the steep slopes of Montaña de Tagoja

Turn left, then right, then climb a concrete track and continue along a grassy track. Turn left as marked up a rugged path on a forested slope and cross the mountain road again, near the Km11 marker. Follow the path up another deep groove in the forest, and cross a grassy track to reach a junction with another track, around 1050m (3445ft) on **Montaña de Tagoja**. The summit rises only a little further to 1089m (3573ft). Turning right along the track leads quickly to the mountain road, while turning left allows a descent to **Santa Cruz**, signposted as the PR LP 3 (see Walk 5, page 48).

WALK 5
Pico de la Nieve to Santa Cruz

Distance	6, 14 or 20km (3¾, 8¾ or 12½ miles)
Start	Mountain road between Km24 and Km25
Finish	Barco, Santa Cruz
Total Ascent	60, 340 or 400m (195, 1115, or 1310ft)
Total Descent	340, 1960, or 2300m (1115, 6430 or 7545ft)
Time	2hr 30min, 4hr 30min or 7hr
Terrain	Rugged mountain paths, steep forest paths and tracks, with some road walking in urban areas towards the end.
Refreshment	Plenty of choice in Santa Cruz.
Transport	None to the start. Buses available around Santa Cruz.

Most walkers climb Pico de la Nieve from a car park, walking there-and-back, leaving afterwards. Those who aren't tied to a car can get a taxi up the mountain road, climb Pico de la Nieve, and/or walk down through forest to Santa Cruz. In effect, there are three options available.

Start high on the mountain road between Km24 and Km25, at a junction with a forest road around 1900m (6235ft). A path signposted PR LP 3 indicates the way to Pico de la Nieve, up wooden steps above the road. Turn left up a slope of pines and broom, where the path is flanked by stones. Reach the end of a forest road and pass a 'parque nacional' sign.

Route uses PR LP 3.

Map continues on pages 46–47

Follow a path drifting high above the forest road, winding up to a junction. Keep climbing as pines give way to broom, drifting

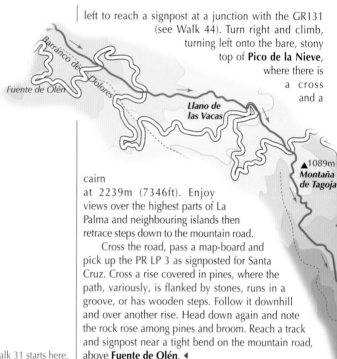

left to reach a signpost at a junction with the GR131 (see Walk 44). Turn right and climb, turning left onto the bare, stony top of **Pico de la Nieve**, where there is a cross and a

Barranco de Dolores

Fuente de Olén

Llano de las Vacas

▲1089m
Montaña de Tagoja

cairn at 2239m (7346ft). Enjoy views over the highest parts of La Palma and neighbouring islands then retrace steps down to the mountain road.

Cross the road, pass a map-board and pick up the PR LP 3 as signposted for Santa Cruz. Cross a rise covered in pines, where the path, variously, is flanked by stones, runs in a groove, or has wooden steps. Follow it downhill and over another rise. Head down again and note the rock rose among pines and broom. Reach a track and signpost near a tight bend on the mountain road, above **Fuente de Olén**. ◄

Walk 31 starts here.

The summit of Pico de la Nieve, at 2239m (7346ft), with El Teide on Tenerife lying far across the sea

Cross the road to continue along the PR LP 3, across a steep slope of pines and broom, descending along a crest and down stone steps to another road bend. Cross over, step down onto a track and follow it down among pines, broom and rock rose. Laurisilva later fills the spaces between pines and the track steepens. Walk straight ahead at a bend, down a steep path with stone steps. Follow another bit of the track then turn left down a grassy track, and quickly right down a path as signposted. Walk down to a track and round a bend, dropping to a bend on the mountain road at **Llano de las Vacas**.

The path descends along a forested crest, crossing a road bend above Fuente de Olén

Turn left down the road, past the Km16 marker, leaving the road as marked at a bend to go down stone steps. Turn right down log steps in a deep, steep groove in dense forest. A steep track leads down to the mountain road, around 1050m (3445ft). Cross over and follow a track a short way

47

to reach a junction with the PR LP 3.1 (which is Walk 4 from Santa Cruz) near the summit of **Montaña de Tagoja**. Keep right to stay on the PR LP 3, Pista Hoyo Tagoja, or Camino del Dorador, for Santa Cruz.

Follow the track down, then over a rise, to a complex junction. Keep right as marked, down wooden steps and a winding earth path on a steep slope of pine and laurisilva. Follow a wall and fence down to a track serving a property on the crest. Cross a rise and descend past a pylon. Apart from a level stretch, the path descends, steep and winding, on the forested crest, becoming rough and rocky. Pines give way to sparse palms, while the scrub features tabaibal, verode, prickly pears, agaves, fennel, calcosas and cornical. The path is easier as it winds down to a road at **El Dorador**.

Turn left along the road, go through a gap in the roadside barrier, and wind steeply down a scrubby slope. Turn right down a concrete road, past bananas, down a rugged path, under a pipeline and down a track in the bed of **Barranco de El Dorador**. Turn right, winding up a stone-paved path, and keep straight ahead, down and up a concrete road. Turn left up a narrow concrete and tarmac road. Go down to a road junction beside a fine dragon tree, turn left down the road to a bus shelter, and cross over as marked. Walk down a bendy stretch, then down to the right, following a stone-paved path into a banana-filled valley.

Turn left down a road, past an ermita, to reach a plaza at the church of Nuestra Señora de La Encarnación, first place of worship built in Santa Cruz. Across the plaza from the church, a narrow zigzag path with stone steps drops downhill. Follow a road down beside a barranco and cross a footbridge to finish at the **Barco**.

WALK 6

Santa Cruz to Puerto de Tazacorte

Distance	31km (19¼ miles)
Start	Plaza de España, Santa Cruz
Finish	Puerto de Tazacorte
Total Ascent/Descent	1500m (4920ft)
Time	9hr
Terrain	Urban and cultivated slopes, steep forested slopes, with plenty of road-walking and urban areas later.
Refreshment	Plenty of choice in Santa Cruz, El Paso, Los Llanos, Tazacorte and Puerto de Tazacorte.
Transport	Buses link Santa Cruz with El Paso and Los Llanos. Buses link Los Llanos with Tazacorte and Puerto de Tazacorte.

The Camino Real de Los Puertos was the first route across the forested Cumbre Nueva, followed by the Refugio del Pilar road, then two road tunnels were cut. The old mule track offers a coast-to-coast walk, although roads have to be used at the start, and more so for the latter half of the route.

Leave the Plaza de España in **Santa Cruz**, climbing as described in Walk 35 to reach the main road at **Cruz de los Bolos**. The GR130 turns left at a crossroads, while the PR LP 1 runs straight ahead up the concrete Camino La

Route uses PR LP 1.

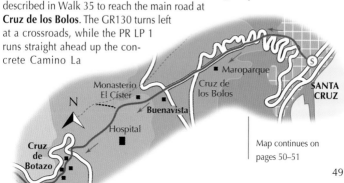

Map continues on pages 50–51

49

Looking back down a well-vegetated path from high above the Hospital

Estrella. Cross another main road near the Restaurante La Graja at Buenavista and walk further up Camino La Estrella. Huge walls guard oranges and date palms, while the **Monasterio del Císter** lies to the right. Further uphill, turn left (straight ahead is Walk 3) and the concrete road gives way to a country track overlooking the **Hospital**. The track is gentle, then steep with chestnuts alongside, dropping to a bend on a busy main road. Cross with care and climb the steep Camino Los Mimbres, passing houses to return to the main road above **Cruz de Botazo**.

Turn left up the main road and bear left down a track past small houses. A grassy path runs down into Barranco de Aguasencio. Pass a junction and climb gently, cross the barranco and wind uphill. The path is stone-paved or rocky among laurisilva and chestnuts, reaching the main road near the Km10 marker. Turn left along the road, crossing to a map-board, then climb a steep path with log and stone steps. The path winds up a slope of laurisilva, with pines at a higher level, on **Lomo de las Vueltitas**.

Pass a stone seat as the path climbs among taller, denser trees to pass another seat. The ascent is relentless and passes five signposted path junctions. Turn right at the first two and left at the next three. Pass a little wayside shrine and the gradient eases, eventually reaching a dirt road on Cumbre Nueva at 1414m (4639ft). ▸ The road is used by the GR131 (see Walk 44) and a monument commemorates this island-hopping route and its incorporation into the pan-European E7 route.

Walk down a broad, rugged,

A small open refuge offers shelter nearby, to the left.

Map continues on pages 52–53

GR131

Lomo de las Vueltitas

Cruz de Botazo

1414m

rgen   N   GR131

stone-paved track, which later winds on a steep slope of pines. Keep straight ahead later, walking to the left of a low drystone wall. Pass an **ermita** and a big pine, and continue down a road, Calle Virgen del Pino, to reach a crossroads. ▸ Continue straight ahead, bearing in mind

Left is for the national park visitor centre, right is for Pico Bejenado and La Cumbrecita (see Walk 15).

that half the distance has been completed, but the rest is almost entirely along roads.

Agaves, eucalyptus and prickly pears line the road as it runs gently downhill. Turn left as marked, and follow the road up past houses and cultivated plots at **La Rosa**. Stay on Calle La Rosa, ahead and downhill, past a junction with Calle del Pino, to a crossroads. Go down Calle La Rosa Cruz Grande, past a shop to reach a pensión. Turn left down Calle General Mola, down through a crossroads and down Calle Manuel Taño into **El Paso** (all services available).

Cross the main street and walk down Calle Paso de Abajo, past a map-board. The road drops steeply, becoming Camino Hermosilla. Pass a restored gateway and restored Fielato de Hermosilla and keep left to go down Calle el Canal. Follow a track beneath the concrete canal as it spans a valley. Follow a track on the left side of the valley, which becomes Calzada Jesús del Monte. Cross a busy main road at **Triana**, where there are bus stops.

Walk down Camino de Triana, noting the GR130 coming in from the left, and later leaving on the right for Los Llanos (see Walk 37). Walk down past bananas and houses to reach a large roundabout. Follow Camino los Palomares past houses and bananas at **Palomares**, keeping left of the Europlátano building. Keep straight ahead at Cuatro Caminos to follow Cuesta Cardón steeply downhill. Cross a busy main road and keep straight downhill. Concrete gives way to tarmac on Calle Cardón, flanked by tall houses, with a brick-paved road leading into **Tazacorte** (all services available).

Keep right of an attractive plaza beside the church and walk down Calle Calvo Sotelo to reach the busy main road. Turn

F Puerto de Tazacorte

Tazacorte

El Arenero

Palomares

Triana

right to follow the road, using a path behind a barrier to reach the Km54 marker. Fork right down a cobbled path, crossing the main road twice. Turn left at the bottom and walk along the sea front into **Puerto de Tazacorte** (all services available). Buses turn in front of Casa del Mar.

Puerto de Tazacorte and its black ash beach is hemmed in by cliffs

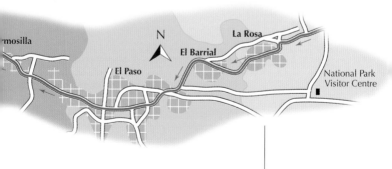

53

WALK 7

El Paso to Refugio del Pilar

Distance	7km (4½ miles)
Start	Centro de Visitantes, El Paso
Finish	Refugio del Pilar
Total Ascent	635m (2085ft)
Time	2hr
Terrain	Roads, tracks and paths, forest and ash slopes.
Refreshment	Possible snack van at Refugio del Pilar.
Transport	Buses serve the Centro de Visitantes from Santa Cruz, El Paso and Los Llanos. Taxi from Refugio del Pilar.

This walk runs from a handy bus route to a forested gap at Refugio del Pilar. This area is a hub for several walks, north along the Cumbre Nueva, south along the Cumbre Vieja, and down to the east coast of La Palma. Use this ascent to link with Walks 8, 9, 10, 11, 14, 44 or 45.

Route uses PR LP 14.

It is possible to walk by road from El Paso, via Tenerra and El Pilar, to reach the start of this walk. If starting from the **Centro de Visitantes** (national park visitor centre), walk carefully down the main road to a crossroads, where the PR LP 14 crosses, passing a lavadero and map-board, around 820m (2690ft). Follow Calle Las Moraditas away from the main road, rising and falling gently, then rising past houses on the slopes of **Montaña Las Moraditas**. Watch for a track flashed yellow/white off to the right, which climbs towards forest and rejoins the road at a higher level.

Enter the Parque Natural Cumbre Vieja and follow the road straight up among pines. Watch for a walled track rising from the road, starting with a couple of stone steps. The track is broad and partly stone paved, later crossing the road. Continue climbing, passing a tagasaste plantation. When the road is joined again the tarmac ends, so follow a stony track further uphill. A few heather trees appear in the forest, while a short-cut uses an old track to avoid a bend on a more recent track. Keep following the old track to cut out more bends, then follow the main track uphill, patched with concrete for a stretch. Climb gently and steeply, passing more and more heather trees, then the forest thins out on broad, bare slopes of volcanic ash.

Keep to the main track, crunching up to a marker post for the PR LP 14. Turn left up a broad ash track and approach a road at **Llanos del Jable**, but don't use it. ▶ A path drifts away from it, flashed yellow/white, up past pines to cross the road at a higher level. ▶ Climb stone steps on an ash slope and follow the winding path into dense pines and heather with lots of moss and lichen.

The path reaches a road with fencing beside it, and a three-way signpost. Walk gently up the road and turn right to enter the recreational area around **Refugio del Pilar**. There is a visitor centre at 1455m (4775ft), with a map-board beyond.

National Park Visitor Centre

Montaña Colorada

Montaña Las Moraditas

N

Montaña Enrique

Montaña Quemada

Llanos del Jable

CR 131

Refugio del Pilar

Nearby Montaña Quemada erupted in 1480.

Walk 14 runs up this road.

Misty pines and heather trees in the forest on the way to Refugio del Pilar

55

WALK 8
Refugio del Pilar to Santa Cruz

Distance	10.5 to 16km (6½ to 10 miles)
Start	Refugio del Pilar (picnic and recreation area)
Finish	Harbour, Santa Cruz
Alternative Finish	Los Cancajos or Breña Alta
Total Descent	1250 or 1550m (4100 or 5085ft)
Time	3hr 30min to 5hr
Terrain	Steep and sometimes rugged forest paths, tracks and roads, giving way to cultivated slopes and urban areas.
Refreshment	Plenty of choice in Santa Cruz, Los Cancajos and Breña Alta. Bars at Breña Baja and El Llanito. Possible snack van at Refugio del Pilar.
Transport	Taxi to start. Buses link Santa Cruz with San Isidro, Breña Baja, Los Cancajos and Breña Alta.

This route runs downhill from Refugio del Pilar, splits and splits again, offering a choice of three finishing points. The PR LP 18 runs all the way to Santa Cruz. The PR LP 18.1 runs to the coastal resort of Los Cancajos. The PR LP 18.2 runs to Breña Alta.

Route uses PR LP 18, PR LP 18.1 and PR LP 18.2.

Leave **Refugio del Pilar**, at 1455m (4775ft), following a road gently up through a cutting. Reach a map-board and dirt road on the left then turn immediately right down a forest path, signposted as the PR LP 18. This drops through pines and laurisilva, landing on a track. The track gives

Map continues on page 59

18.2

Pared Vieja ■

Pista Carbonero

GR 131

Ⓢ

Refugio del Pilar ■

way to a rugged path, winding down through dark, dense laurisilva. There are gaps where trees have been felled to allow clearance for a pylon line. Don't get mixed up with a nature trail, but watch for yellow/white markers to reach a map-board and road at the entrance to the **Pared Vieja** recreational area.

Cross the road and turn left down a track through laurisilva, short-cutting a road bend, and beware of a rock-step onto the road. Continue down a rugged track, reaching another gap in the forest for the pylon line, then there is laurisilva down to a road. Cross over and continue down through laurisilva. Cross a track and walk down to a narrow road and a three-way signpost. Turn right to stay on the PR LP 18 for Los Guinchos. ▸

See later for PR LP 18.2.

The road reaches a junction with a track and another three-way signpost. Turn left down the track, steep and rocky at times, with cultivated plots on either side. Turn right down a concrete track, and when it forks, walk straight between the two branches as signposted, crossing the track on the left to continue down a rugged path. Wind downhill and continue down a concrete track, and just before tarmac is reached, drop to the right on a rocky path. This becomes stony and stone-paved through dense laurisilva, emerging to follow a concrete track towards the **Centro Hipico**. Pass this on a grassy track parallel to a road, reaching the road at a three-way signpost. Turn left onto the road and walk down it for the PR LP 18. ▸ The path runs beside the road in a grassy rut, but isn't easy to follow. A signpost points across the road to avoid a bend at the Km17 marker, then follow the road left to **Cruz de Pavona**. ▸ Turn right down a concrete track and keep straight ahead as marked, avoiding houses, continuing down a broad, steep, stone-paved

See later for PR LP 18.1.

The San Isidro bus turns here for Santa Cruz.

57

The Cruz de Pavona is one of many wayside crosses that are decorated each year on 3 May

track. At Camino El Pino, go straight down a concrete road, veering left as marked down a narrow, walled path. This broadens, becoming steep and stone-paved. A concrete track leads down to a road at Camino la Fuente. Keep straight ahead downhill, past cultivated areas and Cruz del Centro.

At the very bottom, turn left along a road used by the GR130 (see Walk 35), to reach a three-way signpost. Turn right down to a main road in **Breña Baja**, crossing to continue down Camino El Brezal, passing Cruz de Las Ledas. Keep walking downhill, turning left and right to reach another main road. Turn left (PR LP 18 briefly links with PR LP 18.1) and follow the road down to a crossroads at **Cuatro Caminos**. Cross a busy road and go down Camino La Cuesta del Socorro. Avoid turnings off a steep concrete road, which becomes even steeper, then rugged and stone-paved. Later, it passes bananas and lands on a road near the **Ermita del Socorro**. Walk down the road, past bananas, to reach a busy main road.

Turn left to walk up the road until a signpost points right, down a scrubby slope, using the stone-paved Cuesta de la Pata. A road runs down past bananas to a busy dual carriageway at **El Fuerte**. Turn right and note a limekiln while spiralling down and under the main road. Walk down to the coast road and turn left, passing a power station. A promenade path passes **Playa de Bajamar**, popular with evening strollers, joggers and roller-bladers. Vegetation screens it from a busy dual carriageway, and it leads to the harbour in **Santa Cruz**.

PR LP 18.1 to Los Cancajos ▶

Leave the three-way signpost by walking down a concrete track, and keep straight ahead when it rises slightly. Another three-way signpost is reached, so go down the track marked PR LP 18.1. Pass a covered reservoir and go down a track that has concrete and stony stretches, passing a tall fence bounding a cemetery. Walk down the access road

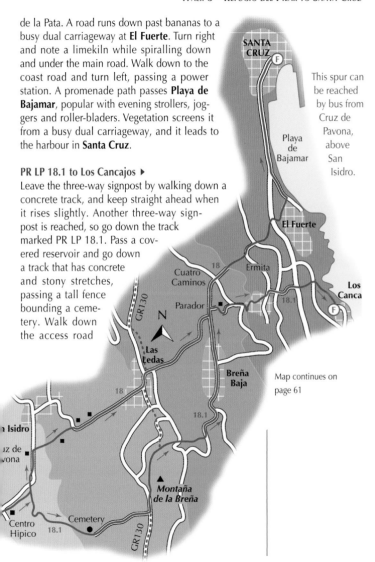

This spur can be reached by bus from Cruz de Pavona, above San Isidro.

Map continues on page 61

Looking towards the well-wooded ash cone of Montaña de la Breña on the way to Breña Baja

from the cemetery to reach a main road used by the GR130 (see Walk 35).

Turn left to follow the road over a gap, where there is a recreational area on the forested slopes of **Montaña de la Breña**. Follow the road up to a junction, then in-between the two roads an ash path is signposted as the GR130 and PR LP 18.1. This rises gently then runs down to a concrete road, reaching a three-way signpost. Turn right along another ash path signposted for Los Cancajos, stony and narrow along a woodland margin, dropping to a road.

Turn left, then quickly right up a steep concrete road, levelling out past a couple of houses. Go down to the end of a tarmac road, along a short grassy path, then down a rugged, stony path. Follow markers, sometimes along a terrace and sometimes along a crest. Land on a road and turn left to follow it gently downhill, past fragrant incienso and eucalyptus. Walk down past a small housing development and turn left at a junction through **Breña Baja** along Calle Felix Duarte Pérez (shops and bars). Pass between the *Ayuntamiento* (town hall) and a chapel on Plaza las Madres.

Stay on the level road, through a crossroads, down the road for San Antonio. Two three-way signposts are passed (PR LP 18.1 briefly links with PR LP 18), so turn right at the second through the grounds of the luxury **Parador** hotel. Leave along its access road with fine views of its Canarian garden. Turn right down a main road and watch for a signpost on a bend. Turn left down a narrow ash path on a wonderfully scrubby slope, with a few palms and a fine dragon tree near the bottom.

Enter a little car park to find the path flashed yellow/white through a paved area with seats. Walk down past dragon trees to reach a road. Turn left along Camino de El Tonolero, then right past bananas. Turn right again and cross a very busy main road to reach a bus shelter, then go down a quiet road past more bananas. Cross another busy main road and pass the Restaurante El Cantillo to walk down a quiet road. Walk off the end, down steps, across another road and down lots of concrete steps. Follow a promenade path past black ash beaches to a bus stop at **Los Cancajos** (resort with all services).

PR LP 18.2 to Breña Alta

Leave the three-way signpost by turning left along the tarmac road, Pista Carbonero, then right as signposted for El Llanito, down an old, narrow road. When the tarmac ends, continue down a rugged, walled track. Cross a concrete road and quickly short-cut to a tarmac road. Cross

The PR LP 18.2 runs down cultivated slopes, passing little farm buildings, to finish in Breña Alta

this and walk down a path into laurisilva, winding downhill, the path stone-paved at times, to reach the road again. Drop down into laurisilva again and the rugged path becomes a good track, leading to a concrete track. Turn left down the walled track to reach the road again.

Turn right down the road, watching for two tracks leaving it on the left, both close together. Go down the second, or narrower, past woods and fields, then the stony track changes to a narrow tarmac road as it drops. Pass a circular concrete reservoir, and keep left as marked down a clear track, past barking dogs. Go straight down a rugged track, straight along a concrete track, downhill from Finca Nogales. Laurisilva is mixed with cultivated areas and rampant mixed scrub. Walk down to a bend on a road at **La Traviesa**.

The cross is another that is decorated on 3 May.

Keep walking down, passing Cruz del Manchón. ◄ Walk straight down Camino El Manchón, on tarmac and concrete, past Cruz de La Sociedad. Walk down to a junction on a bend where there is a three-way signpost at **La Sociedad**. At this point the PR LP 18.2 joins the PR LP 19. Continue down Camino La Piedad, referring to Walk 2, to finish at **Breña Alta**.

WALK 9

Refugio del Pilar to Playa del Hoyo

Distance	15km (9½ miles)
Start	Refugio del Pilar
Finish	Playa del Hoyo or the airport
Total Descent	1455m (4775ft)
Time	4hr 30min
Terrain	Forest paths and tracks, steep and rugged at times, giving way to roads and tracks on cultivated slopes.
Refreshment	Bars off-route at Mazo, Playa del Hoyo and the airport. Possible snack van at Refugio del Pilar.
Transport	Taxi to start. Buses serve Mazo from Santa Cruz and Fuencaliente. Buses serve the airport from Santa Cruz.

This Camino del Faya runs downhill from Refugio del Pilar, through pine forest and laurisilva onto cultivated slopes. A steep descent on attractive stone-paved roads leads close to Mazo. The route continues down to the rugged coast at Playa del Hoyo, only a short walk from the airport.

Leave **Refugio del Pilar**, at 1455m (4775ft), from a mapboard behind the visitor centre. The PR LP 17 is signposted

Route uses PR LP 17.

Part of the extensive recreational site among pine forest at Refugio del Pilar

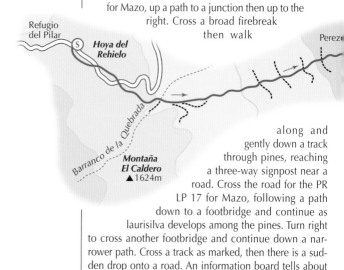

for Mazo, up a path to a junction then up to the right. Cross a broad firebreak then walk along and gently down a track through pines, reaching a three-way signpost near a road. Cross the road for the PR LP 17 for Mazo, following a path down to a footbridge and continue as laurisilva develops among the pines. Turn right to cross another footbridge and continue down a narrower path. Cross a track as marked, then there is a sudden drop onto a road. An information board tells about the faya trees (Myrica faya) that flourish here.

Cross the road to continue down through forest, crossing a track twice as signposted, continuing down to a footbridge and a track in the **Barranco de la Quebrada**. Turn left, gently up the track, until a lesser track is signposted down to the left. Pass a couple of buildings and the viewpoint Mirador del Camino de la Faya. Further down, a path runs left down to a three-way signpost. Keep left, down into dense laurisilva, passing a multi-trunked heather tree covered in lichen. Emerge further down where markers steer the route down a track. Follow this until another signpost indicates a left turn down a rugged path, which becomes broader and easier, passing an almond plantation.

Continue down a rugged track and later step to the left along a bit of old path. If this is missed, a signpost later indicates a right turn off the track in a clear-felled area. The path has some stone-paved stretches as it runs down through laurisilva, and there are stone walls alongside. Cross a couple of tracks and always keep straight

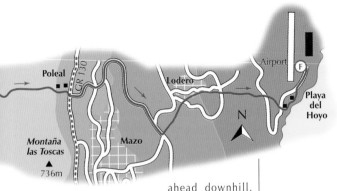

ahead downhill.
A signpost eventually points right, down a clear track to a road at **Perezquillo**.

Walk towards a gateway and turn right down into laurisilva. A rugged path leads to a track and more signposts. SL (*senderos local*) routes head right and left, while the PR LP 17 runs downhill for Mazo. Follow a rugged old stone-paved path through laurisilva, where clearings appear bit by bit, full of flowers and grass. Avoid all turnings, but at one point when a grassy track crosses, make a quick right and left turn. Continue down a narrow path through fragmented laurisilva and the path broadens, reaching a concrete track at a signpost. Either walk down the track, or take little short-cuts through a couple of bends, to a three-way signpost at **Poleal**.

The GR130 is encountered here (see Walk 35), and a right turn leads to a complex road junction, map-board and a confusing three-way signpost. However, simply walk straight down a steep and narrow road, down a rugged track and down a concrete track marked 'Camino la Faya'. Land on a main road at a Km5 marker and bus shelter, and cross over to follow Camino la Montañeta steeply downhill. Turn left at a junction and wayside cross and continue downhill. The road bends right as it falls, rises gently, then runs down to a main road and bus shelter far below **Mazo**.

Turn right up the main road and fork left down a concrete track as flashed yellow/white. Pass vines and walk down an old, grassy, stone-paved track down to a road. Cross over and go down a concrete road near **Lodero**,

The end of Walk 9 is the rugged coast near Playa del Hoyo, not far from the airport

then a grassy, stone-paved track, keeping right down to a road. Keep right at a junction to continue downhill, with vines and houses alongside. Cross a road and go straight down a concrete track, Camino los Palitos, which becomes rough, stony and stone-paved later, passing vines, scrub and a banana tent. Turn left down a concrete road past more bananas, reaching a bus depot.

Cross a road and go down the road marked 'excepto bus', passing bananas to reach a busy road. Cross over to reach the rocky coast at **Playa del Hoyo**. Turn left to find the Restaurante Casa Goyo among huddled huts. If transport is required, walk up the road to reach the **airport**, where there are buses, taxis and bars.

WALK 10

Refugio del Pilar to Playa del Hoyo or La Salamera

Distance	15km (9½ miles)
Start	Refugio del Pilar
Finish	Playa del Hoyo or La Salamera
Total Ascent	150m (490ft)
Total Descent	1700m (5575ft)
Time	5hr
Terrain	Forest tracks and paths, then steep cultivated areas with roads and tracks. Options to descend to the coast.
Refreshment	Bars at Mazo, Playa del Hoyo and La Salamera. Possible snack van at Refugio del Pilar.
Transport	Taxi to start. Buses serve Mazo from Santa Cruz and Fuencaliente. Buses serve Malpaises from Santa Cruz.

This route runs downhill from Refugio del Pilar and splits, with one spur dropping to Mazo, reaching the coast at Playa del Hoyo, and the other dropping to La Salamera. There is a small village at La Salamera, but no bus service, so a pick-up needs to be arranged.

Leave **Refugio del Pilar**, at 1455m (4775ft), from a map-board behind the visitor centre. The PR LP 16 is signposted for Mazo, up a path to a junction then up to the right. Cross a broad firebreak then walk along and gently down a track through pines, reaching a three-way signpost near a road. Turn right up a track signposted PR LP 16, rising among pines with a sparse understorey of heather. Stay on the main track, avoiding others, passing a bare slope and later levelling out on a gap beside **Montaña El Caldero**. Descend and turn round the snout of a rugged, mossy lava flow. The pines thin out, leaving heather, broom and rock rose. Reach a track junction and signpost at **Llano de las Moscas**. ▶

Route uses PR LP 16 and PR LP 16.1.

Walk 11 continues straight ahead.

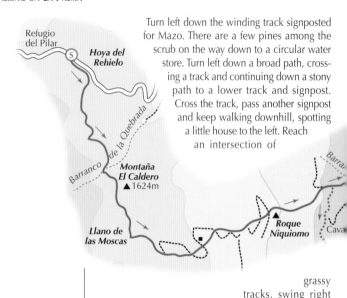

Turn left down the winding track signposted for Mazo. There are a few pines among the scrub on the way down to a circular water store. Turn left down a broad path, crossing a track and continuing down a stony path to a lower track and signpost. Cross the track, pass another signpost and keep walking downhill, spotting a little house to the left. Reach an intersection of grassy tracks, swing right and climb a little. At the next track junction, turn left as signposted for Mazo, winding gently down to another signpost. Drop down a path through dense laurisilva, crossing a track to continue downhill. The path becomes steep and rugged, reaching a junction close to **Roque Niquiomo**.

Walk straight downhill, the path rugged at first, then easier along a narrow forested crest. Look back to see Roque Niquiomo, and spot it again while passing a grassy clearing. Turn right down a steep track, back into woods and down to a signpost. Go round a bend at a junction of tracks to find another signpost pointing left for Mazo. ◀

Turning right leads to La Salamera (see later).

A rugged, wooded path leads down to a concrete track. Go straight down it to a junction and walk straight through a gap as marked, down a grassy path. Watch for markers, avoiding paths into adjacent fields. Eventually reach a track and turn left to follow it a short way down to the bed of **Barranco Cordero**. Walk down the rocky bed and cross a track close to a road bend. Walk down the barranco a bit

68

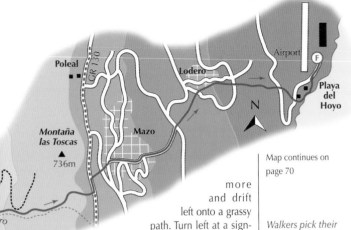

Poleal

GR 130

Lodero

Airport

F

Playa del Hoyo

N

Montaña las Toscas
▲
736m

Mazo

Map continues on page 70

more
and drift
left onto a grassy
path. Turn left at a signpost for Mazo and right to continue down beside little fields. The path
is flanked by heather and bramble scrub, heading down to a track.

Walkers pick their way down a rocky but easy barranco above Mazo

Walk down the track, but watch for a turning on the right, down an ash and pumice path. Cross a road and follow another short path down to a road junction and three-way signpost. The GR130 is encountered here (see Walk 36), so turn left to follow it down to another three-way signpost below a recreational area on **Montaña las Toscas**. Turn right and walk straight downhill on various surfaces to reach the main road in Mazo (bank with ATM, post office, shops, bars, buses, agricultural and craft markets). The walk can end here, or continue downhill to link with Walk 9 to the coast.

Cross the road and walk down a splendid, steep, stone-paved road. Pass a plaza beside the Ayuntamiento and walk

69

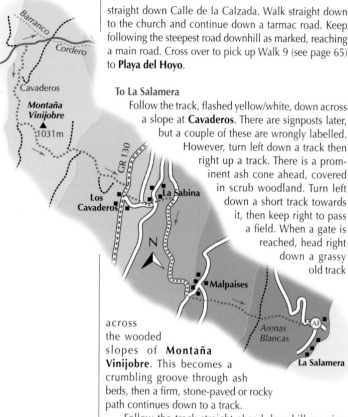

straight down Calle de la Calzada. Walk straight down to the church and continue down a tarmac road. Keep following the steepest road downhill as marked, reaching a main road. Cross over to pick up Walk 9 (see page 65) to **Playa del Hoyo**.

To La Salamera

Follow the track, flashed yellow/white, down across a slope at **Cavaderos**. There are signposts later, but a couple of these are wrongly labelled. However, turn left down a track then right up a track. There is a prominent ash cone ahead, covered in scrub woodland. Turn left down a short track towards it, then keep right to pass a field. When a gate is reached, head right down a grassy old track across the wooded slopes of **Montaña Vinijobre**. This becomes a crumbling groove through ash beds, then a firm, stone-paved or rocky path continues down to a track.

Follow the track straight ahead downhill, passing heather and tagasaste. Watch for a left turn down a path, which cuts a bend from the track. Walk straight down the track to reach a road and signpost at **Los Cavaderos**. The GR130 (Walk 36) crosses here, so turn right to follow it, then turn left at a wayside cross to leave it. Walk down a broad, stone-paved old road, down a road as signposted, and down a short stone-paved track to reach a main road near **La Sabina**. There is a bus shelter to the left, but to continue the route, either cross the road or go beneath it.

Walk straight down a narrow road on a steep, stony, dusty slope and follow an old paved path down to another road. Turn right to follow it past a few houses and gardens, heading down, up a bit, then down again. Watch for a left turn down a narrow road, Camino de Eusebio, reaching a main road near a shop, bar and bus shelter at **Malpaises**. Cross the road to go down a narrow road or track, Camino las Maretas. This drops to another road beside a small wayside cross. Go straight down another track, and when this turns left, go straight ahead down a narrow path, past one last house.

A steep, rugged, stone-paved and stone-strewn path cannot be hurried. Follow it down slopes rampant with mixed scrub, crossing a dirt road further downhill. A stony, dusty track leads down scrubby slopes at **Arenas Blancas**. Hit a bend on a dusty track and continue down the path, noting cardón. A final steep and rugged slope leads to a road, and the road is easily followed to the little village of **La Salamera**, dominated by a tall lighthouse. There is a refreshment kiosk and a bar, but no buses.

Looking down a steep, scrubby and rugged slope from Malpaises to La Salamera

WALK 11

Refugio del Pilar and Pico Nambroque

Distance	12km (7½ miles)
Start/Finish	Refugio del Pilar
Total Ascent/Descent	350m (1150ft)
Time	4hr
Terrain	Forest tracks and mountain paths, rugged on the ascent, easier across ash slopes on the descent.
Refreshment	Possible snack van at Refugio del Pilar.
Transport	No public transport.

This circular route from Refugio del Pilar wanders through pine forest and climbs towards Pico Nambroque. A diversion off-route allows a view of the enormous crater of Hoyo Negro. A stretch of the Ruta de los Volcanes leads across forested ash slopes to return to Refugio del Pilar.

Route uses PR LP 16, SL VM 125 and GR131.

Start by following Walk 10 away from **Refugio del Pilar**, to reach the track junction and signpost at **Llano de las Moscas**. Walk ahead as signposted SL VM 125, gently up a track to another junction and signpost. Turn right and follow the track onwards, well to the left of a large building, climbing and winding up through forest. Avoid all turnings and stay on the main track, climbing round a forested crater below **Montaña de la Morcilla**, reaching a turning circle.

Turn left up the track, which is rather stony and sometimes narrow, but follow it up past steep agglomerations of bouldery lava. Watch for a right turn up an indistinct path, rough and rocky at times, with stone steps climbing above the forest onto an ash slope. Only a few pines and sparse scrub are dotted around, and the path contours across the shoulder of **Pico Nambroque** to reach the crest around 1875m (6150ft). There is a three-way signpost where the GR131, or Ruta de los

Walkers stride along an easy forest track at Llano de las Moscas

Volcanes, crosses. ▶ Turn right to follow the GR131 down a stony ash path, past pines to cross a footbridge over a gully. Wander up and down across a slope of pines and bare ash, crossing the flank of **Montaña de los Charcos**. Head down among pines where broom and rock rose grow. Walk down the path to reach a three-way signpost on the flank of **Montaña la Barquita**. Keep left downhill through pines, following an

Turn left to visit the crater of Hoyo Negro.

Refugio del Pilar

Hoya del Rehielo

dor del rigoyo

Pico Birigoyo

N

Montaña la Barquita

Barranco de la Quebrada

Montaña El Caldero ▲1624m

Montaña de los Charcos

Llano de las Moscas

GR131 1875m

Montaña de la Morcilla

▲ Pico Nambroque

A signposted path junction on the slopes of Pico Nambroque

Walking straight
downhill quickly
links with Walk 14.

easy forest track. When it leaves the forest it crosses a
steep slope of broken lava on the flank of **Pico Birigoyo**.
Reach another three-way signpost. ◄ Turn right as signposted GR131, up across a slope of ash and rocks, with
only a few pines. Turn a corner to head downhill and
there are more pines, as well as tagasaste bushes. A final
three-way signpost offers an ascent of Birigoyo, otherwise continue down among dense pines, with a view
available from **Mirador del Birigoyo**. The path is broad
and clear as it winds down to a map-board and signpost
at the visitor centre at **Refugio del Pilar**.

WALK 12
Jedey to Tigalate

Distance	22km (13½ miles)
Start	Jedey
Finish	Tigalate
Total Ascent	1230m (4035ft)
Total Descent	1130m (3710ft)
Time	6hr
Terrain	Mostly good paths and tracks on forested ash slopes, but some parts are steep and rugged.
Refreshment	Bar and shop at Jedey and Tigalate.
Transport	Buses serve Jedey and Tigalate from Santa Cruz, Fuencaliente and Los Llanos.

Forest paths and tracks link Jedey and Tigalate, little villages on either side of the Cumbre Vieja. There are bare ash slopes on the higher parts, where the route crosses a gap between volcanic cones. The route signposted varies significantly from the route shown on maps.

Start at the bar in **Jedey**, around 600m (1970ft), walking towards a shop and pizzeria. Turn left up Calle Campanario, neither signposted nor waymarked. Follow the road up past a little school then turn left as flashed yellow/white up a pumice path flanked by low walls. Quickly cross the road on a lava flow, then follow the path up among pines. Climb past slopes of vines in the forest, and when an ash depression is reached, swing left as marked, following a track over a slight rise. Turn right to pass in front of a house and follow a rocky path across a slope of pines. Emerge on an ash slope and follow the path on a gently rising traverse. Avoid left turns and the path later winds up among dense pines.

Cross a track above a vineyard and keep climbing, although with a couple of short descents across little

Route uses PR LP 15.

75

barrancos. Climb until a track is reached and turn right to follow it out of the forest at **Los Guanches** to pass little buildings, vineyards and tagasaste. Avoid turnings to properties and follow the track back into forest. Keep to the main track, avoiding one climbing left, but later watch for a yellow/white flash and a couple of little cairns where a rough and stony path climbs left. Follow this to link with a much smoother track up the forested slope.

The track winds uphill, passing an old iron barrier, catching glimpses of a steep and rugged lava flow outside the forest. Climb straight up the lava flow later to reach a junction. Turn right gently down a track across a slope of pines and broom. Reach another junction and signpost, turning left up past a barrier for the PR LP 15. Long and lazy zigzags climb gradually uphill, with occasional glimpses of very steep, stony slopes outside the forest. A narrow ash path continues up a stony slope of pines. Climb and later drift right up a bare grey ash slope. Peep into a shallow grey ash crater while turning left near **Montaña Nueva**, but note how the ash cones high above are red. Pass a couple of signposts on the way to an

intersection of paths on an ash gap, **Collado de las Deseadas**, at 1828m (5997ft).

The PR LP 15 crosses the GR131 (see Walk 45). Head down an ash track signposted for Tigalate, swinging left and levelling out at **Llano de los Guanches**. Follow yellow/white flashes and a signpost, and later watch for

76

a marker revealing an ash track down across a slope of pines. Turn right as signposted at a junction, where stones have been pushed aside to mark a steep path down the forested slope. The path reaches a track and marker post not far from the **Refugio de Tigalate**.

Slopes of black ash give way to the red ash cone of Volcán Deseada

Cross the track and continue downhill, the path vague at first, then flanked by stones, becoming steep and rugged. Cross the track a couple more times,

Llano de s Guanches
m

Refugio de Tigalate

Pista de la Morriña

F

Tigalate

then there is a long and steep descent before another track is crossed, where there are buildings to the right. Keep walking downhill and cross the track again. The path is broader, even stone-paved, but still rough. The

The route crosses the Collado de las Deseadas and intercepts the GR131 (Walk 45)

pines thin out and heather trees are abundant. Cross the track again and walk down a grassy track, still rugged in places. Watch for markers to go down a scrubby slope dotted with houses, huts and water tanks, reaching a signpost at a road-end.

The GR130 crosses here (see Walk 36), so turn right to follow it, but almost immediately turn left to follow the Camino Viejo down to a main road. Turn right into the little village of **Tigalate**, around 700m (2295ft), where there is a bar, shop and bus shelter. If a bus isn't due, consider walking down the Camino Tigalate to the church below the village, for a different bus service.

WALK 13

San Nicolás and Coladas de San Juan

Distance	10km (6 miles)
Start/Finish	San Nicolás
Total Ascent/Descent	600m (1970ft)
Time	3hr
Terrain	Roads, tracks and steep, rugged paths on forested and cultivated slopes.
Refreshment	Bars at San Nicolás.
Transport	Buses serve San Nicolás from Santa Cruz, Los Llanos and Fuencaliente.

In 1949 a volcanic eruption sent a lava flow down towards the village of San Nicolás. Fortunately, it split and passed on both sides. This route explores areas that were covered by the lava, and areas that were spared. The circuit can be extended by linking with Walk 14.

Leave **San Nicolás**, around 600m (1970ft), walking up a road, Carretera San Nicolás, signposted for Tacande. Watch for an ash track on the right, onto rugged black lava. A PR LP 14.1 signpost is hidden in a pine tree. Apart from a bit of tarmac, the track is ash and stone, steepening as it climbs. Look right to see the **Ermita Virgen de Fatima**, built where the lava flow split around the village. Step over a pipe

Route uses PR LP 14.1.

79

and climb among a few pines. Cross another pipe and climb past pines and vines, then walk up a concrete track, eventually reaching a picnic site at **Los Pelados**.

Climb straight up a narrow, walled path, join a track and follow it uphill, avoiding two turnings with chains across them. Watch for yellow/white flashed short-cuts, first up to the right, then turn right up a concrete stretch of track. Take a short-cut up to the left, climb round a concrete bend and follow the track up to the next sharp bend. Turn right up an ash track, still among pines, in a valley with a few vines and scrub. Walk up a track, but switch to a narrow ash and pumice path climbing directly up the valley, crossing the track twice. The last part of the ash path reaches a three-way signpost. ◄

Turn left to link with Walk 14.

A rugged black lava flow, dating from 1949, stopped against pine forest at Coladas de San Juan

Turn right along an easy path across a slope of pines to reach another signpost, at around 1130m (3710ft). A cobbly path leads gently down a barren lava flow at the **Coladas de San Juan**. Keep to the path and marvel at smooth and ropy lava flows. The path drops into and climbs from a gully where the lava fractured as it drained and cooled, and there are views up to the Cumbre Vieja. A signpost is reached on the other side, where a right turn starts the descent.

The path is on rugged lava at first, then drifts into dense pines. There are other signposts on the slope, always pointing downhill along forest tracks or various paths. The path becomes steep and dusty, winding down past pines with tagasaste among them later. The path is rough and stony on a scrubby slope, running down past vines to more signposts at **Llanos de Tamanca**. ▶ Turn left to follow a winding road downhill, passing vines most of the way down to the main road at the Km39 marker. Either turn left along the road to finish in **Jedey**, or turn right to return to San Nicolás. The return uses part of the GR130 (Walk 37), following the Camino Tamanca down from the main road. Keep right at a junction and watch for a path climbing back to the main road at a wayside shrine at Km40. Follow the main road back into **San Nicolás** to finish (shops, bars and buses).

There is an option to turn left up a track, signposted SL EP 107, for Hoyo de la Sima. This is 1.5km (1 mile) with a climb of over 400m (1310ft), reaching a fearsome deep hole in the mountainside. See Walk 14.

WALK 14

Llanos del Jable and Coladas de San Juan

Distance	11km (7 miles)
Start/Finish	Llanos del Jable
Total Ascent/Descent	600m (1970ft)
Time	3hr 30min
Terrain	Tracks and paths, steep and rugged at times, on forested slopes and ash slopes.
Refreshment	None
Transport	No public transport.

Slopes of volcanic ash have either remained bare or have been colonised by pines on this circuit. At Coladas de San Juan the route also crosses a barren lava flow, dating only from 1949. If using buses for access, approach this route using Walk 7 or Walk 13.

Route uses SL EP 104, SL EP 105, PR LP 14.1 and SL EP 103.

There is a small car park at **Mirador de Los Llanos del Jable**, around 1340m (4395ft) on a road near Refugio del Pilar. Follow an ash track from the mirador, flashed green/white, to a three-way signpost. Turn left for the SL EP 104, climbing an ash path, joining a track and turning right. When the track briefly levels out at a junction among pines, keep left, and when it levels out again, turn left up a path on an ash slope. Climb into dense pines where the path winds steeply, flashed green/white. Cross a forested gap, around 1600m (5250ft), beside **Montaña del Gallo**.

Keep left uphill to link with Walk 10.

Descend from the pines across ash and rocks, reaching a junction with a track at a three-way signpost. ◄

Following the bendy track onwards leads to a fearsome deep hole in the mountainside at Hoyo de la Sima.

Turn right downhill as signposted SL EP 105. The track runs into forest and bends right. Watch for a signpost on the left, indicating a lesser track zigzagging downhill. Land on a forest track and turn left to follow it across a slope of pines, soon looking down on an awesome chasm of lava. Walk further along the track and watch for a marker indicating a path down to the right. ◄

Walking on the forested ash slopes below Volcán Bernardino

A narrow path zigzags down a slope of dense pines. Pick up the line of an old path and follow it down beside the chasm of lava. The path is rugged and reaches signposts for the PR LP 14.1, linking with the course of Walk 13. Turn right to follow a path into and up from a gully where the lava fractured as it drained and cooled. There are views up to the Cumbre Vieja, and the path is marked gently up and across a barren lava flow at the **Coladas de San Juan**. Keep to the path and marvel at smooth and ropy lava flows.

Pass a signpost where the lava gives way to a slope of pines. An easy path leads across the slope to a three-way signpost. Keep straight ahead as signposted SL EP 103, along a gently undulating rising traverse. The slope bears pines, broom and rock rose. Join a track and keep walking ahead, avoiding a track climbing right, and another dropping left. Rise to another three-way signpost on the slopes

Montaña Quemada ▲
Llanos del Jable
Mirador ●
SF
Volcán Bernardino
Montaña del Gallo ▲
1611m
GR 131
Coladas de San Juan
Hoyo de la Sima ●

83

Bare ash slopes and sparse pine forest on the way across Llanos del Jable

of **Volcán Bernardino**. Keep straight ahead and down the track, round a little valley where chestnuts grow among pines. The pines thin out as the ash track rises and falls, passing masses of tagasaste and mixed scrub later. When passing a concrete hut, fork left downhill as flashed green/white, into denser pines to reach a track junction.

Turn right as signposted SL EP 103, following the ash track as it winds gradually up across slopes of pines. These thin out, leaving barren slopes of ash, although mosses, lichens and tiny plants survive. Keep climbing past a couple of marker posts, where Walk 7 comes up from El Paso. Keep right to approach a road at **Llanos del Jable**, but don't use it. ◄ A path drifts away from it, flashed yellow/white, up past pines to reach the road at a higher level. Turn right to follow the road uphill, winding past the Km5 marker, where heather grows among pines. Finish back at **Mirador de Los Llanos del Jable**.

Nearby Montaña Quemada erupted in 1480.

CALDERA DE TABURIENTE

The highest mountains on La Palma overlook a very deep and steep-sided, canyon-like valley called the Caldera de Taburiente. This is protected as a national park, and as it is surrounded by unstable rock faces and scree slopes, scored by dozens of barrancos, there are only a couple of access

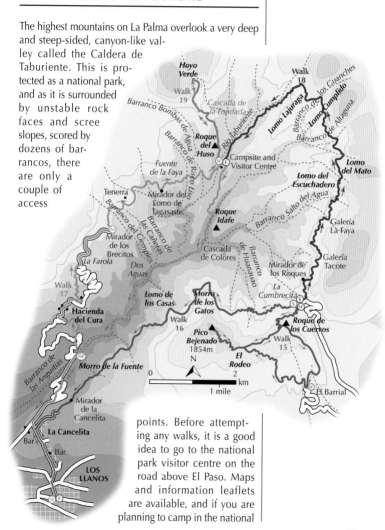

points. Before attempting any walks, it is a good idea to go to the national park visitor centre on the road above El Paso. Maps and information leaflets are available, and if you are planning to camp in the national park, a permit must be obtained from the centre (free of charge). The national park website contains plenty of useful information and maps.

Walks 15, 16, 17, 18 and 19 enter the national park, with Walk 15 offering splendid views of the Caldera from the summit of Pico Bejenado. Walk 16 links the two roads serving the park, from La Cumbrecita and Los Llanos. The most popular access into the Caldera is covered in Walk 17, and note the provision of four-wheel drive taxis that allow this route to be shortened. Bear in mind that Walk 18 is particularly difficult and access might well be denied, but experienced, sure-footed walkers, with a good head for heights tend to agree that there is no finer route into the Caldera. Walk 19, although fairly short, is so remote that it can really only be covered by those willing to camp in the heart of the Caldera de Taburiente – which is highly recommended.

For more information see the national park website, www.gobiernodecanarias.org/parquesnacionalesdecanarias/en/CalderaTaburiente.

A lava tube beneath a lava flow on the approach to Pico Bejenado (Walk 15)

WALK 15
Pico Bejenado

Distance	8 or 10.5km (5 or 6½ miles)
Start/Finish	La Cumbrecita or El Barrial
Total Ascent/Descent	600 or 800m (1970 or 2625ft)
Time	3 or 4hr
Terrain	Mostly good tracks and rugged paths, sometimes on very steep forested slopes.
Refreshment	None
Transport	No public transport.

Most mountains on La Palma shoulder each other up, with very few standing in isolation, but Pico Bejenado rises proudly above Caldera de Taburiente. To avoid a long road-walk from the national park visitor centre, it is best to climb from road-ends at El Barrial or La Cumbrecita.

There are two possible starting points, La Cumbrecita and El Barrial. If drop-offs and pick-ups can be arranged, it is possible to walk between one and the other. The climb from La Cumbrecita uses a very steep zigzag trail, marked 'solo expertos' (experts only) on one steep slope. The climb from El Barrial is on an easier forest track and rugged path, marked as the PR LP 13.3, which can be combined with other paths and tracks to form a circuit.

Route uses PR LP 13.3.

From La Cumbrecita
Leave the stone-paved car park at **La Cumbrecita**, at 1305m (4280ft). Pass a barrier to follow a track and almost immediately climb up a path on the left, zigzagging up a steep slope of pines and rock rose. The path is fenced later and stone-paved steps climb a cliff. Keep climbing then zigzag downhill. Traverse a steep forested slope then zig-zag uphill, later passing a fence where a cliff is covered in houseleeks. Wooden steps climb to a junction near

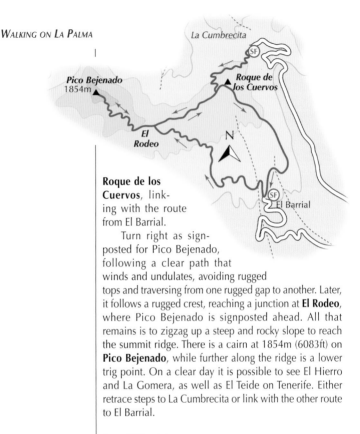

Roque de los Cuervos, linking with the route from El Barrial.

Turn right as signposted for Pico Bejenado, following a clear path that winds and undulates, avoiding rugged tops and traversing from one rugged gap to another. Later, it follows a rugged crest, reaching a junction at **El Rodeo**, where Pico Bejenado is signposted ahead. All that remains is to zigzag up a steep and rocky slope to reach the summit ridge. There is a cairn at 1854m (6083ft) on **Pico Bejenado**, while further along the ridge is a lower trig point. On a clear day it is possible to see El Hierro and La Gomera, as well as El Teide on Tenerife. Either retrace steps to La Cumbrecita or link with the other route to El Barrial.

From El Barrial

The start can be reached by car, following Calle Valencia and continuing along a dirt road, Pista de Valencia, to a small car park and map-board at 1150m (3775ft). Leave **El Barrial** by following the dirt road towards Pico Bejenado. Rise across a sparsely forested slope and pass a large sign for the Parque Nacional de la Caldera de Taburiente. Turn left, bearing in mind that the track on the right is used later for the return. Almost immediately there is a fork, so keep left on the clearest track and climb gently, crossing little barrancos. ◀ Lava tubes can be seen in rock cuttings beside the track.

The PR LP 13.3 trail climbs to the dirt road from El Paso.

Looking back across La Cumbrecita shortly after starting the climb towards Pico Bejenado

Watch for a path signposted on the right, climbing a slope of pines and rock rose. Zigzag up to a junction, where a short detour right leads to a petroglyph, or rock engraving, reaching an enclosure containing a boulder carved with a vague, wavy line. Continue up the main path, climbing long, lazy zigzags at a gentle gradient among sparse pines. Turn a rocky corner and climb to a rocky gap on the ridge. Keep left and a little further up the ridge is **El Rodeo**, where there are views down into Caldera de Taburiente. All that remains is to zigzag up a steep and rocky slope to reach the summit ridge. There is a cairn at 1854m (6083ft) on **Pico Bejenado**, while further along the ridge is a lower trig point.

Retrace steps to **El Rodeo**, then either continue straight back to El Barrial, or keep left along another path to vary the return. Follow the rugged crest and the clear path that winds and undulates, avoiding rugged tops and traversing from one rugged gap to another. A junction is reached, where left is signposted for La Cumbrecita, 'solo expertos' (experts only), while straight ahead is signposted for Pista de Valencia. Climb up and along the forested, bouldery crest to reach another junction close to **Roque de los Cuervos**. Turn right downhill, following a forested crest. Later, continue along a forest track and always stay on the clearest track at junctions, to be led back to **El Barrial** and the car park on Pista de Valencia.

WALK 16
La Cumbrecita to La Cancelita and Los Llanos

Distance	12km (7½ miles)
Start	La Cumbrecita
Finish	Los Llanos
Total Ascent	600m (1970ft)
Total Descent	1555m (5100ft)
Time	7hr
Terrain	Steep, forested slopes and cliff faces. Narrow paths are sometimes exposed and crumbling.
Refreshment	Plenty of choice in Los Llanos.
Transport	Taxi to start. Buses serve Los Llanos from most parts of La Palma.

This linear route traverses the northern slopes of Pico Bejenado, following narrow paths across steep forested slopes, using even narrower, crumbling paths across cliff faces. It needs care throughout its length, due to the ever-present danger of rock-fall and might be closed in bad weather.

Leave the stone-paved car park at **La Cumbrecita**, at 1305m (4280ft), and pass a barrier to follow a track towards Mirador Lomo de las Chozas, gently down and up to a worn gap. The Sendero Cumbrecita-Cancelita, a national park trail, heads left. Follow it down into forest and cross two footbridges close together. Continue down to cross a third, then down again to cross a fourth. Zigzag uphill and traverse easily round to the **Barranco de Huanauao**. Cross over and climb lots of steep zigzags, before turning a corner and heading downhill. Roque de la Zarza and Pico Bejenado loom overhead, while the path runs down into another forested barranco. As the ground becomes bare, the path is narrow and crumbling, crossing patches of rock-fall debris.

Route uses the Sendero Cumbrecita-Cancelita.

    Cross Fuente de la Zarza and make a gentle rising traverse on a forested slope. Drop to pass Fuente de las Brujas and cross patches of rock-fall. Climb and drop steeply a short way, then make a gentle rising traverse to a pronounced corner. The path runs down along a ridge, making a sharp left turn leading further down. Pass beneath cliffs at **Morro de los Gatos** then zigzag down a ridge away from them. Another sudden left turn leads to the base of more fearsome cliffs.

The path is narrow and needs care as it passes below cliffs that are gradually crumbling

    Stay on the narrow, rock-strewn path, which exploits a crumbling, thin, grey layer of rock, with unstable cliffs above. Follow a downward traverse, broken by a gully full of rock-fall debris. Climb steeply a short way then go down a crumbling, narrow path. Cross an awkward wet and vegetated patch then take care down a steep, crumbling path. A narrow path runs across and down a forested slope. The next cliff pushes the path down **Lomo de los Casas**, out onto a rocky ridge, turning sharply back again. A rising traverse between cliffs and a very steep forested slope is

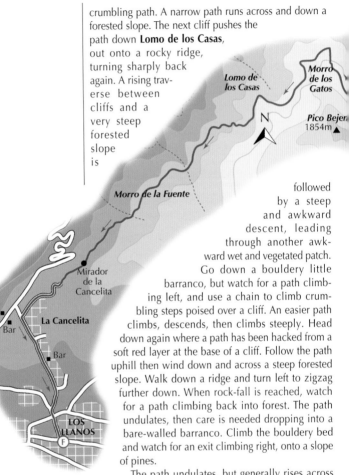

followed by a steep and awkward descent, leading through another awkward wet and vegetated patch. Go down a bouldery little barranco, but watch for a path climbing left, and use a chain to climb crumbling steps poised over a cliff. An easier path climbs, descends, then climbs steeply. Head down again where a path has been hacked from a soft red layer at the base of a cliff. Follow the path uphill then wind down and across a steep forested slope. Walk down a ridge and turn left to zigzag further down. When rock-fall is reached, watch for a path climbing back into forest. The path undulates, then care is needed dropping into a bare-walled barranco. Climb the bouldery bed and watch for an exit climbing right, onto a slope of pines.

The path undulates, but generally rises across a rocky, forested slope with cistus bushes. A long, winding path drops to a patch of laurisilva. The path undulates gently, climbing among pines, then descends among almonds and prickly pears. Later, the path is uncomfortably loose, dusty and stony. A water channel could be followed across a cliff face, but it is better to follow a path far below it, across a scrubby slope. Climb to the **Mirador de la Cancelita**, at 600m (1970ft), and enjoy a last look back at the steep, forested slopes.

Walk down a track and turn left down a road, Calle Cancelita, then left again down a road flanked by bananas and avocados, passing houses. Calle Lomo de los Caballos changes to Camino la Caldera and a bar is passed. Always keep straight ahead along roads, through a complex junction, to reach **Los Llanos**. Pass a paved area and sports pitch, following the wide Calle Conrado Hernandez and its narrow continuation, to La Plaza Chica and the church in the town centre.

WALK 17

Barranco de las Angustias and Caldera de Taburiente

Distance	14 or 27km (8¾ or 16¾ miles)
Start	Los Llanos or Los Brecitos
Finish	Los Llanos or Barranco de las Angustias
Total Ascent	200 or 1400m (655 or 4595ft)
Total Descent	1080 or 1400m (3545 or 4595ft)
Time	4hr 30min or 9hr 30min
Terrain	Roads, tracks and a variety of paths, often on steep slopes of scrub or forest. Paths towards the end are rugged and can flood after rain.
Refreshment	Plenty of choice in Los Llanos.
Transport	Taxi shuttles run between Barranco de las Angustias and Los Brecitos in the mornings.

This is a long walk if started and finished in Los Llanos, but the distance can be halved, walking only from Los Brecitos to the Barranco de las Angustias, which is mostly downhill. This is the easiest way to explore the Caldera de Taburiente, but by no means an easy walk.

Route uses PR LP 13.

Start at the church in **Los Llanos**, walking behind it to La Plaza Chica. Follow the narrow Calle Conrado Hernandez and continue straight ahead down a wide road, through a complex junction. The PR LP 13 is signposted, and a right turn shortly afterwards is signposted for Caldera de Taburiente.

Map continues on page 97

Walk up a road, past bananas and avocados, turning left up Camino La Caldera. Pass a bar and continue straight up Calle Lomo de los Caballos. Turn right at the highest road junction to walk down through two rock cuttings. A path is signposted left down log steps on a scrubby slope. Cross the road and go down a short, steep path. Cross the road again and go down a steep path. Walk down the road from a hairpin bend and drop left as signposted down a partly stone-paved path. Cross the road and short-cut another bend. Turn right down the road to reach a car park in the **Barranco de**

Hacienda Del Cura

ASF

Morro de la Fuente

Barranco de las Angustias

Mirador de la Cancelita

La Cancelita

Bar

Bar

LOS LLANOS

SF

94

las Angustias. ▶ To walk and climb to Los Brecitos, cross a paved ford and turn right upstream, then turn left up to a three-way signpost. Turn left again to follow a path climbing, steep and stony, across a slope of scrub and pines. Cross the road and go up a few steps, climbing a steep, winding path and log steps back to the road. Cross over and follow a stone-paved path uphill and left. Cross a track and follow a path up to a junction, where a note is painted on a boulder reminding walkers that the fruit is private! Pass the boulder and later turn left to follow a winding concrete track up slopes of fruit.

Before reaching the last house, turn left up a winding path, passing a few pines and scrubby slopes to reach a road bend. Turn right up the road, round the bend and round a hairpin bend. Scrubby slopes of tabaibal, calcosas and prickly pears give way to avocados and a huddle of houses at **Hacienda del Cura**. Cross a barren slope to reach a stand of pines beside the road, and turn left up a track. Climb past tangled tabaibal, calcosas, tagasaste and prickly pears, with vines, oranges and figs in places. The track serves a few houses, then a path climbs in long zigzags past scrub, pines and vines.

Climb into pine forest with a prickly pear understorey, reaching a clearing. Two tracks fork, but don't follow them. Keep left up a path, following a water pipe up through the forest. The path is steep, winding, stony, loose and dusty, reaching a hairpin bend on a road at **La Farola**. Follow the road across a forested slope to reach a car park and viewpoint at **Los Brecitos**. ▶ Follow a fenced path down across a slope of pines and patchy laurisilva. Climb a little then walk gently down across four footbridges, the last across **Barranco del Ciempies**. Climb past pines, tagasaste and heather, then cross a footbridge over **Barranco de las Cañeras**. Follow the path across a slope and catch a glimpse of a farm at **Tenerra**, and continue downhill. Pass a massive boulder, heather trees and willow in Barranco de las Traves. Follow the path down and cross a footbridge over Barranco de las Piedras Redondas, passing huge boulders. Cross a forested slope and descend to **Mirador del Lomo de Tagasaste**.

4km (2½ miles) have been covered, and this is where the taxi shuttles meet walkers bound for Los Brecitos.

This is 6km (3¾ miles) from the Barranco de las Angustias, at 1080m (3545ft), at the end of the road for the taxi shuttles.

Crossing the bouldery Playa de Taburiente to the campsite and visitor centre in Caldera de Taburiente

Petroglyphs can be visited off-route as signposted, climbing to two inscribed boulders in a fenced enclosure.

Zigzag down and cross a slope of pines and laurisilva, then zigzag down to a footbridge across **Fuente de la Faya**, where a damp slope bears lush vegetation. There is a good view while turning a corner and the path descends easily across a slope of pines. Cross a footbridge over **Barranco de Risco Liso**, and follow the path across a forested slope. ◀ Zigzag down to cross the bouldery **Barranco Bombas de Agua**, then the path undulates but generally descends, reaching a junction where Hoyo Verde is signposted left (see Walk 19). Turn right to boulder-hop across **Río Taburiente** and cross a couple of streams among willow to climb to a campsite among pines, heading for a stone-built national park visitor centre.

A path leaves the visitor centre, signposted for Barranco de las Angustias. It undulates and crosses a gap with fine views, as there are later at a corner at Somada del Palo. A narrow path slices across a steep slope, then zigzags to drop steeply on a slope of pines and broom, with views of the pinnacle of **Roque Idafe**. Reach a junction where left is signposted 'salida por atajo', for experts, and right is 'salida normal', the way most walkers go. Both paths join at Las Lajitas del Viento. Walk down through the

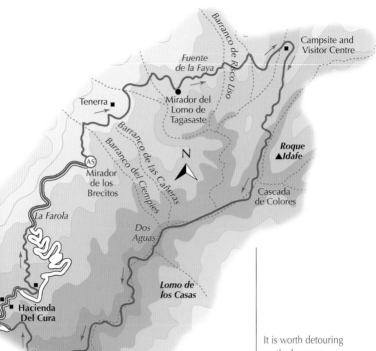

Barranco de Risco Liso

Campsite and Visitor Centre

Fuente de la Faya

Barranco de las Cañeras

Tenerra ■

Mirador del Lomo de Tagasaste

Roque ▲Idafe

Barranco del Ciempies

(AS)
Mirador de los Brecitos

Cascada de Colores

La Farola

Dos Aguas

Hacienda Del Cura ■

Lomo de los Casas

It is worth detouring up the barranco to see iron-stained waters at **Cascada de Colores**.

barranco, passing Cruce de Barrancos and an altar. ▶

Walk down the pebbly riverbed almost to a water intake building at **Dos Aguas**, where two rivers converge. The path runs on the opposite bank to the building and it is best to follow signposts and waymarks. Later, drop back into the riverbed near a small concrete building. Further downstream, pass under a water pipe that looks like a footbridge. A path heads up to the left, dropping back into the riverbed, but watch for another path climbing left above the rocky gorge. When this drops again, go round a rocky corner and take the 'privateweg' on the right to avoid a rocky scramble and/or deep water.

Back in the riverbed, a path climbs left and later drops. Climb on the right, high above the gorge, passing

Walkers deep in the Barranco de las Angustias returning to the roadside car park

a little stone building at Morro de la Era. Cross a water channel and drop to the riverbed for a while, passing under a concrete arch. Watch for a signposted path up to the left, which later zigzags back to the riverbed, crossing a rock lip in front of a gorge, climbing the other side. Cross Barranco de la Fraile, and drop to the main riverbed later.

Simply walk down the broad, cobbly bed, but watch for a path rising on the left and follow it a short way. Cross the riverbed to continue downstream, with houses in sight. Squeeze past boulders and follow the bouldery bed under a concrete arch, then a track rises left. It soon drops back into the riverbed, and a paved ford is reached where the route crossed **Barranco de las Angustias** earlier in the day. Follow the road to a car park, at 200m (655ft). If you parked here, the walk is over. To return to **Los Llanos**, retrace the earlier steps of the day.

WALK 18
La Cumbrecita to Caldera de Taburiente

Distance	13km (8 miles)
Start	La Cumbrecita
Finish	Campsite, Caldera de Taburiente
Total Ascent	500m (1640ft)
Total Descent	1060m (3480ft)
Time	7hr
Terrain	Narrow, crumbling paths on very steep and unstable slopes. Danger of rock-fall and landslide. Chains are fixed on many awkward stretches.
Refreshment	None
Transport	No public transport. Taxi to start and walk out.

This is probably the most dangerous walk in this book, and access might be denied. The path is literally falling apart so check its condition in advance at the national park visitor centre. However, it also offers the most scenic, dramatic and exciting access to the Caldera de Taburiente.

Leave the stone-paved car park at **La Cumbrecita**, at 1305m (4280ft), passing a national park information kiosk. Check if the path is open, and even if it is, park staff may dissuade you. Follow the path down and along a short ridge to a map-board under the rocky prow of Punta de los Roques. A zigzag path leads down to a junction, where most walkers turn left for the view from **Mirador de los Roques**, while a path climbing right is signposted for the Zona de Acampada. ▶

Route uses PR LP 13.1.

The campsite is directly below, but there is no direct access.

Follow the path up a steep slope of pines and rock rose, pass through a little notch and zigzag downhill. A water channel is buried beneath the path, which is narrow, stony, gritty, exposed and not suitable for vertigo sufferers. Pass beneath a fang of rock and weave in and out of gullies. The path narrows and must be followed with great care. Go down and up steps where the water channel can't be followed safely, and pass a building near **Galería Tacote**.

The slope bears more forest cover, while the path remains narrow and exposed. A water pipe spans a ravine, where a chain is fixed to the rock. Pass a tunnel mouth and building at **Galería La Faya**. The path becomes awkward as it turns round crumbling buttresses and gullies. There is a gradual ascent, then a steep descent with a chain. ◀ Turn into the bouldery **Barranco Salto del Agua**, where the Zona de Acampada is, unbelievably, signposted straight uphill. The path weaves between boulders, marked by little cairns, with cliffs above. Watch for the path heading left, climbing along

Casual walkers turn back here.

Lomo Lajuraga

Barranco de los Guanches

Lomo Cumplido

Barranco de Altaguna

Río Taburiente

Ⓕ Campsite and Visitor Centre

Lomo del Mato

Lomo del Escuchadero

Barranco Salto de Agua

N

Galería La Faya

Galería Tacote

Mirador de Los Roques

100

La Cumbrecita Ⓢ

the foot of a cliff, crossing slopes of rubble. Scramble on rock later, using a chain, to reach **Lomo del Escuchadero**. Look ahead from a rocky gap to see leaning towers of rock. The path zigzags down a slope of pines and rock rose to cross Barranco Limonero. Rise and fall gently on the slope beyond, then zigzag down the forested **Lomo del Mato**, using a chain on the way into the next barranco, where there might be a waterfall.

The view ahead from Lomo del Escuchadero reveals jagged peaks and leaning towers of rock

Chains assist climbing from the barranco and the path runs through more pine forest. Turn a corner on Lomo de Las Goteras and take care on the descent as the path is steep and slippery. Pass Fuente Prieto, where there is a chain, then further downhill the path is again awkward. Four lengths of chain help on the drop into the bouldery **Barranco de Altaguna**. Scramble across and traverse a crumbling slope to reach a junction. Galería de Altaguna is just downhill, otherwise zigzag up the steep, forested slope. Continue along the base of a cliff to reach a rocky ridge at **Lomo Cumplido**.

A short descent uses a chain, then slopes of rubble lie beneath a cliff. After passing a rocky point things are a little easier as the path crosses a forested slope. Take

The path crosses the deep, rocky cleft of Barranco de los Guanches with the aid of chains

great care on the way down into the awesome, sheer-walled **Barranco de los Guanches**, where the slopes are loose and broken. A couple of chains are available on the way down, and the crumbling paths on the other side also have chains. An easy stretch across a forested slope leads to **Lomo Lajuraga**, followed by a zigzag descent. An awkward chained path crosses steep, unstable slopes, reaching a junction. Galería de Las Verduras de Alfonso is up to the right, otherwise head downhill.

Zigzag down the forested slope, crossing a stream and catching glimpses of waterfalls. Reach a map-board beside a river on the wide, bouldery Playa de Taburiente. Follow the riverbed, where there may or may not be water. Pick whatever seems the best way while enjoying views around the Caldera de Taburiente skyline. Looking ahead, willow scrub fills the riverbed, but before it is reached, a ramp rises on the left among pines. Walk through the *zona de acampada*, or **campsite**, to a national park visitor centre at 750m (2460ft).

The route takes a long time to complete, and suits those who intend camping. If an exit is required there are two options, based on Walk 17. The ascent to **Los Brecitos** is only an option if you can arrange to be collected. The direct descent to the car park in **Barranco de las Angustias** is 8km (5 miles).

WALK 19
Caldera de Taburiente and Hoyo Verde

Distance	6.5km (4 miles) there-and-back
Start/Finish	Campsite, Caldera de Taburiente
Total Ascent/Descent	700m (2295ft)
Time	4hr
Terrain	Steep and rugged paths on forested and rocky slopes.
Refreshment	None
Transport	None

This is only a short walk, but it is very steep and quite rugged in places. It is really only an option for those who are using the campsite in the Caldera de Taburiente. The route climbs to Hoyo Verde, where waterfalls splash through a deep, rock-walled barranco.

Leave the **campsite** in the Caldera de Taburiente and follow signs for Los Brecitos. Cross a couple of streams among willow and boulder-hop across **Río Taburiente**. Reach a path junction and turn right as signposted for Hoyo Verde, rising gently to another sign-posted junction. Turn left and climb a zigzag path beneath the cliffs of **Roque del Huso**. One part has a chain and a fence alongside. Climb past a gap and follow the path up a rocky ridge, again with a chain and a fence alongside. Pass a damp patch where the vegetation is lush and green.

Follow the path up a boulder-strewn valley among pines and cross where marked

Route uses a national park trail.

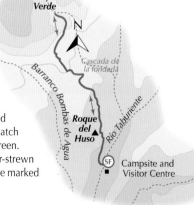

Looking back beyond Roque del Huso, across the Caldera de Taburiente to Pico Bejenado

by a cairn. Climb further and cross back near some enormous boulders. A fence is reached at a gap, overlooking the slender waterfall of Cascada de la Fondada. Keep climbing and follow a zigzag path up a steep slope of pines, grappling with boulders at one point, where there is an understorey of heather. Later, climb a bouldery gully as marked by little cairns, reaching a ridge where there are signs close together, overlooking **Barranco Bombas de Agua**.

Follow the path signposted for **Hoyo Verde**, climbing a steep slope of pines and heather. Cross rocky areas then traverse where a weak layer causes an overhang at the base of a cliff. This is a remarkably flowery terrace in spring. The path is awkward in places, so take care. Pass a mirador sign, at over 1400m (4595ft), and follow a vague path down into the Barranco de Hoyo Verde. Scramble up or down to see rock pools and little waterfalls, but be sure to retrace steps back to the **campsite**, as there is no other exit.

WALK 20

Tijarafe and Porís de Candelaria

Distance	10km (6¼ miles)
Start/Finish	Tijarafe
Total Ascent/Descent	850m (2790ft)
Time	3hr 30min
Terrain	Steep and rugged paths, tracks and roads.
Refreshment	Bars in Tijarafe.
Transport	Buses serve Tijarafe from Los Llanos and Puntagorda.

A path drops steeply from Tijarafe, down scrubby slopes to the coast at Porís de Candelaria. After crossing to nearby Playa del Jurado, another path zigzags uphill and the ascent continues through cultivated slopes to El Jesús. A stretch of the GR130 returns to Tijarafe.

Follow the road from **Tijarafe**, around 640m (2100ft), towards Puntagorda. Go round a bend and left along Calle Acceso al Colegio, passing a college and a shop. Follow the road ahead and downhill, flashed yellow/white, branching right down a track signposted for Puntagorda, past almonds. Turn left down a stone-paved track to reach a road, cross over and follow another road, signposted downhill for Porís de Candelaria. Fork left along another road and walk down a concrete road to **Casaquemada**.

Route uses PR LP 12.2 and GR130.

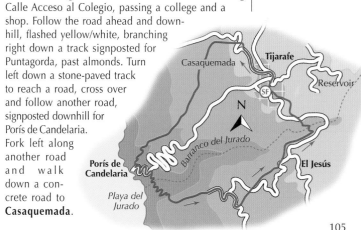

A winding, partly restored, stone-paved track drops to the sea at Porís de Candelaria

The road turns right, but turn left instead down a short, rugged path.

Walk straight down another concrete road and straight down a rough and rocky path. Follow a rib of rock down a scrubby slope, cross a track and continue downhill. Turn left at a palm tree, and into a rocky dip to cross a gentle valley. The path runs easily past a few pines, generally on a gentle downhill traverse. The scrubby slopes are tangled with cornical, with patches of tabaibal, verode, prickly pears and a few almonds. The path begins to drop, becoming more steep and rugged, crossing lumpy rock and loose stones.

The path appears to head for a cliff, but turns left downhill, past more tabaibal before it reaches a steep drop. A plain and obvious, very convoluted zigzag path can be seen, and while some parts are rugged, other parts have been restored, and lots of cardón grows on the rugged slopes. The path doesn't reach a car park, as might be expected, but drops almost to the sea at **Porís de Candelaria** before climbing to the car park. ◀

The little settlement of huts is reached by a short detour.

106

Follow a zigzag concrete road uphill, past a mirador. There are no short-cuts on the way to a small parking space on a gap. ▶ The road climbs to Tijarafe, but the route continues down steps signposted for Playa del Jurado. The path zigzags interminably downhill at a gentle gradient, but needs care as the slope is steep, loose, gritty and dusty. Pass beneath an overhang and pass odd little buildings at the bottom, among masses of calcosas and tabaibal at **Playa del Jurado**. This settlement was once served by a cable, whose pylons are seen on the opposite side of the barranco.

The only exit is a path zigzagging up a steep slope. This is firm, but still stony and dusty, passing under the old pylon line six times as views open up along the **Barranco del Jurado**. Reach a mirador at the top and turn left as signposted for Tijarafe, up a concrete road towards banana tents. However, turn left again to follow a rugged path uphill, following the old pylon line, keeping left of a banana tent to follow the rocky, scrubby edge of the barranco further uphill. At another banana plot, a track on the right leads to a road. Turn left to follow the winding road, which keeps changing from tarmac to concrete, reaching a junction. ▶

Turn right and walk gently down the bendy road as marked. Turn left up a very steep concrete road in a cutting. Keep left of a house and climb a narrow, rugged path. Cross a road and keep climbing, passing houses, huts, water storage tanks, cultivated and scrubby slopes. Join and follow a concrete road up to a tarmac road beside the little church at **El Jesús**. There is a three-way signpost, where the GR130 could be followed right to reach a bus stop, or left to return to Tijarafe (see Walk 38)

Stone steps can be used to climb a rocky little peak.

The route varies from that shown on some maps.

WALK 21
Tinizara to Piedras Altas and Tijarafe

Distance	15km (9½ miles)
Start	Tinizara
Finish	Tijarafe
Total Ascent	1000m (3215ft)
Total Descent	1250m (4100ft)
Time	5hr
Terrain	Mostly quiet roads, forest and farm tracks, with steep paths up and downhill.
Refreshment	Bars at Tinizara and Tijarafe.
Transport	Buses serve Tinizara and Tijarafe from Los Llanos and Puntagorda.

In the past, travellers crossed the highest parts of La Palma, using a network of trails linking all the villages around the island. Two trails are combined on this walk, one climbing above Tinizara, linking with another at Piedras Altas to descend to Tijarafe.

Route uses PR LP 12.1 and PR LP 12.

Tinizara is a scattered settlement, so start at the Restaurante Tinizara, around 900m (2950ft), and walk down the road towards Tijarafe. Watch for a map-board on the left, where a path flashed yellow/white climbs from the road. This is stone-paved, then concrete as it passes a few houses. Continue straight up a road, watching for a path rising like a ramp on the left. This cuts a bend from the road, and the road is crossed later. A broad, stone-paved path climbs steeply past a few more houses, reaching pines. Fork right, cross a track and follow a track to the right of some vines, into tall pine forest. The **Llano de El Lance** recreational area is to the left, with an information hut.

Climb a steep track beside terraces, up past pines, broom and rock rose, clipping a road bend. Continue straight up the track, almost clipping another road bend. Follow a concrete track up a slope of vines, figs and almonds. Turn right up a tarmac road and right up a concrete track as marked. This cuts out a bend and the road is followed again, levelling out for a while. Climb again and turn right up a concrete track, rising steeply to reach a cross-track at the **Refugio de Tinizara**, beside a menagerie of 'rare breeds' at 1330m (4365ft). ▶

La Traviesa, Walk 22, crosses here.

Keep straight ahead uphill, signposted PR LP 12.1, through the forest and up another steep slope of vines. The concrete ends where a track crosses. Climb a path between more vines, the highest being well over 1500m (4920ft). The path is broad, but narrows on the rocky ridge of **Lomo de las Piedras Altas**, where boulders have

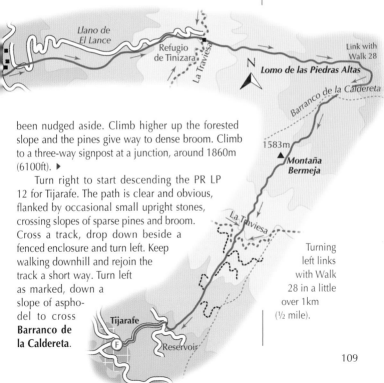

been nudged aside. Climb higher up the forested slope and the pines give way to dense broom. Climb to a three-way signpost at a junction, around 1860m (6100ft). ▶

Turn right to start descending the PR LP 12 for Tijarafe. The path is clear and obvious, flanked by occasional small upright stones, crossing slopes of sparse pines and broom. Cross a track, drop down beside a fenced enclosure and turn left. Keep walking downhill and rejoin the track a short way. Turn left as marked, down a slope of asphodel to cross **Barranco de la Caldereta**.

Turning left links with Walk 28 in a little over 1km (½ mile).

An important signposted junction at Piedras Altas, high
on the mountainside at 1860m (6100ft)

The path climbs and descends, with open spaces between
the pines. Reach a path junction, keeping straight ahead
as signposted for Tijarafe. Curve round the forested hump
of **Montaña Bermeja** and start a long, winding descent
down a forested ridge with broom and rock rose. Pass a
signpost while crossing a path ◀ and continue down to
cross a forest track.

La Traviesa, Walk 22,
crosses here.

The forest thins as the path runs further down. Walk
down a track beside vines and keep straight ahead when
the track bends left. Go down a rocky nose, cross a concrete track and continue down as marked. A rugged path
leads down to a concrete road. Turn left down it, but at a
pronounced left bend, drop down to the right as marked.
A rugged path runs down a forested slope where cistus grows. Leave the forest, cross a road, and go down
a rocky path along a scrubby ridge, passing a couple of
ruined casetas. Pass pines to reach a pylon, and turn right
down a rocky path and a concrete track to reach a road
beside a covered **reservoir**.

Turn left to pass the reservoir and follow a new road
winding downhill, reaching the church belfry in **Tijarafe**.

Turn left down steps beside the belfry, left again at the bottom to walk down a brick-paved road, to reach the main road, around 640m (2100ft). Interesting sculptures stand in the Jardín de los Verseadores. (Banks with ATMs, post office, bars, shops, buses and taxis).

Descending through a clearing in the pine forest high above Tijarafe

WALK 22
La Traviesa – El Time to Briesta

Distance	30km (18¾ miles)
Start	Mirador El Time
Finish	Kiosko Briesta (**Note** No accommodation available)
Total Ascent	1330m (4365ft)
Total Descent	630m (2065ft)
Time	8hr
Terrain	Steep forested and cultivated slopes, criss-crossed by narrow roads, tracks and paths. A few paths are steep and rugged.
Refreshment	Bar at El Time and at Briesta.
Transport	Buses serve El Time from Los Llanos and Puntagorda.

In the past, travellers either climbed high mountains to cross La Palma, or stayed low on convoluted mule tracks across rugged barrancos. La Traviesa offered a route across the mid-slopes, not too high, with fewer deep barrancos to cross. It takes two days to follow across remote slopes.

Route follows GR131 and PR LP 10.

See Walk 43 for the route description.

Leave the **Mirador El Time**, around 500m (1640ft), and follow the GR131 uphill, to around 1000m (3280ft), where a PR LP 10 signpost points left for La Traviesa to Briesta. ◄ The path undulates and winds across a forested slope with mixed undergrowth. Follow it round a barranco and drop to a track. Walk down the track, turn right up another track, then go down a path on the left. This winds down into a barranco, drops further, then climbs past a cave. The path runs in and out of three barrancos, where almond terraces are overwhelmed with scrub.

Climb to little buildings and a track at **El Gánigo**. Turn left round a valley thick with prickly pears and dotted with palms, and go up past a little house called La

Cabaña. Turn right up a road, and left to leave it, signposted PR LP 10 both times. Walk up a stone-paved path past old buildings and follow a grassy path round an almond terrace, climbing to a road. Turn left up the road, quickly reaching wayside crosses and a junction at **Llano de la Cruz**. The road descends to El Jesús.

Cross the road and pass Casa Cruz del Llano. Walk along a grassy track which descends easily into a forested barranco. Follow the track up the other side, where it is boulder-paved. Pass below the restored **Fuente de Trajocade**, keeping left and turning a corner into another barranco. An easy path traverses it, then a rough and rocky path climbs and turns into the next forested barranco. Again, an easy traverse crosses it and a rugged path climbs from it, steep and stone-paved, up to a track. Turn right up the track, then left up a stone-paved path. An easy undulating path crosses a very steep forested slope, with occasional fencing alongside. Drop into the **Barranco de Jieque** to face a sheer cliff.

Turn left downstream, cross as marked then zigzag up to a track. Turn right up the track to reach a junction with another track, then watch for a path climbing steeply, rejoining the track at a higher level. Climb a zigzag path as signposted, over 1200m (3940ft). The path makes a gentle traverse and crosses **Barranco de La Tranza**. Leave along another traverse, round a small barranco, then round a ridge where there is a four-way signpost. La Traviesa crosses Walk 21, so keep ahead and later descend to a forest track.

Turn right to follow the track, with a water pipe alongside, roughly contouring in and out of little valleys, crossing the

Map continues on page 115

Looking back down the course of the GR131 before reaching the start of the PR LP 10

big **Barranco de la Caldereta**. Stay on the main track, passing a cave, then a covered reservoir. Turn left down a path as marked, round a valley, then across a slope of vines. Cross a track and follow a forest path on **Lomo la Castellana**. The path is sometimes rugged, mostly climbing, crossing a track and continuing as marked. Curve round a valley, up across a track, then up a path as signposted. Pass between pines and almonds to reach a track, turn right uphill between pines and terraces, then up through pines to a junction.

Turn left down and up a track as marked, through a cross-track and down again. Turn left as marked up a vague, winding path on the forested slope. Reach a house and don't walk up a concrete road, but fork left to walk beside a vine trellis, back into forest. Cross a track and follow the path up to a junction. Walk straight ahead, gently down a track, swing left up a rugged stone-paved track, then walk between a fence and pines. Reach a cross-track at **Refugio de Tinizara**, beside a menagerie of 'rare breeds' at 1330m (4365ft). ◄

Walk 21 crosses here.

114

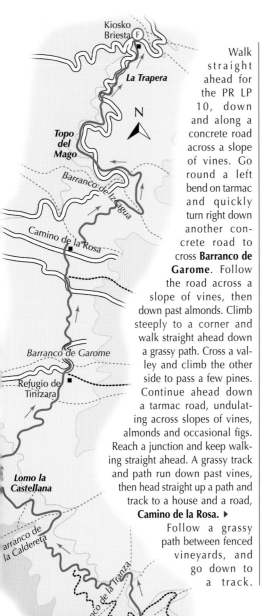

Walk straight ahead for the PR LP 10, down and along a concrete road across a slope of vines. Go round a left bend on tarmac and quickly turn right down another concrete road to cross **Barranco de Garome**. Follow the road across a slope of vines, then down past almonds. Climb steeply to a corner and walk straight ahead down a grassy path. Cross a valley and climb the other side to pass a few pines. Continue ahead down a tarmac road, undulating across slopes of vines, almonds and occasional figs. Reach a junction and keep walking straight ahead. A grassy track and path run down past vines, then head straight up a path and track to a house and a road, **Camino de la Rosa.** ▶

Follow a grassy path between fenced vineyards, and go down to a track.

Walk 28 crosses here.

115

A stretch of fenced path running above a road after leaving the Barranco de Izcagua

Turn right into forest, walking quickly and easily round a valley, reaching a junction. Turn right uphill, then soon afterwards, left downhill. A pleasant track leads through a rock cutting, then turn right as marked, following a track across a deforested slope, back into forest. Turn right down a stony track which is very rugged by the time it reaches the bed of **Barranco de Izcagua**. Cross over and follow an easier path down the barranco, later fenced as it traverses a steep forested slope above a road. Cross a slight gap and walk down a track beside a stout stone wall, reaching a few buildings beside the road.

Turn right to follow the road as signposted. ▸ Turn left down a path as marked, passing almonds on the way into pine forest, then back up to the road near **Topo del Mago**. Walk along the road and later step down to the left, following another path running parallel. Don't follow the RT Traviesa, but head uphill. Go down across a concrete track into a forested valley, passing a signpost. Walk ahead and left to cross a streambed, follow a broad stone-paved path up past a ruin, turning right at the top to return to the road. Walk down the road as signposted, but when it starts climbing, fork right as marked up a path and down to the road again. Follow the road and watch for two more options to follow paths on the right, instead of the road, finally reaching a road junction beside the **Kiosko Briesta**. ▸

Don't follow the 'RT Traviesa' signs.

La Traviesa continues to Barlovento on Walk 23.

WALK 23
La Traviesa – Briesta to Barlovento

Distance	32km (20 miles)
Start	Kiosko Briesta
Finish	Barlovento
Total Ascent	660m (2165ft)
Total Descent	1270m (4165ft)
Time	8hr
Terrain	Steep forested and cultivated slopes, criss-crossed by narrow roads, tracks and paths. A few paths are steep and rugged.
Refreshment	Plenty of choice in Barlovento.
Transport	Buses serve Barlovento from Garafía and Santa Cruz.

La Traviesa continues around the northern mid-slopes of La Palma. The route is not always based on traditional paths, but relies on links provided by more recent forest and farm tracks. As before, the trail is remote and there are no facilities along the trail until Barlovento is reached.

Route uses PR LP 20.

Looking across forested slopes above the clouds before the Barranco de las Grajas

Start at the **Kiosko Briesta**, around 1200m (3940ft), where the PR LP 20 is signposted for Barlovento. A fenced path drops into a forested barranco and a level path turns a corner to cross the main Barranco de Briesta. Climb back to the road, cross over and climb fenced steps. Turn right at a junction and zig-zag up to a three-way signpost, turning right to cross a track and contour into a barranco. Cross the bed above a pipe and climb. Turn right up a track and left along another track that undulates past vines, pines and cabins.

Cross a road and go down another winding track. ▶ Turn left and right along other tracks as marked. A grassy track avoids a farm and enters forest, running straight ahead at a junction. Watch for a path down to the right, following a fence and dropping into **Barranco de las Grajas**, among pines and patchy laurisilva.

Cross the lip of a dry waterfall and follow the path across a grassy slope. Go down through pines and laurisilva to a track. Turn right up it and follow an overgrown path above a house, walking beside a fence. Cross a grassy track and follow a narrow, overgrown path across a slope of grass, heather and asphodel. Pass a house to reach a farm track and turn right up to a concrete track. A signpost points into a mass of thistles, then the path is flanked by heather trees, reaching a track. Turn left as marked, then quickly right, through a gate and over a water pipe. Walk down among pines and laurisilva to a track in the **Barranco del Cedro**.

Turn right to cross the bed and follow the track up to a junction. Keep left and follow the track round to the bouldery **Barranco Barbudo**.

The road climbs to Roque de los Muchachos.

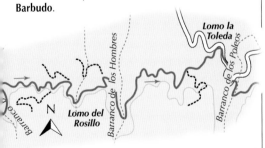

Map continues on pages 120–121

Cross it and climb log steps, zigzag up to a track and turn left gently uphill. When the track runs downhill, turn right as signposted, rising and bending to another junction. Turn

Walking among tall pines in the Reserva Natural Integral Pinar de Garafía

Walk 27 crosses here.

left and head down, reaching yet another junction. Turn right along an undulating track, keep right at a junction further along, and a bendy stretch leads down to another signposted junction, leaving the Reserva Natural Integral Pinar de Garafía. ◄

Keep right, in effect straight ahead, walk round a left bend, and immediately fork right at a junction. Follow the track past a building, down across a concrete bridge over **Barranco de los Hombres**, to a three-way signpost. Climb a concrete stretch and continue along the gentle forest track. Keep right at a junction, turning in and out of a couple of valleys. At a later junction, keep left, winding down from the forest across slopes of scrub woodland with occasional big pines. Reach a road and mirador at **Lomo la Toleda**.

Turn right to follow the road down and round **Barranco de los Poleos**, past pines and laurisilva. After crossing a bridge, turn right up a track, winding up a forested slope. ▶ A marker indicates a right turn, and a path climbs, levelling out later. It descends across a steep slope with fencing alongside, sometimes climbing to reach the bed of **Barranco del Adernero**. Climb a short way to find a path turning sharp left, climbing further to leave the barranco. Later, it turns right and levels out, around 1300m (4265ft). A rising and falling traverse crosses a forested slope to a track.

Turn left down the track to reach a junction and signpost. The winding track basically contours, reaching another junction and marker post. Fork left to follow the track down a steep ridge of scrub woodland, looking ahead to spot a refugio. Keep straight ahead at a junction, then right down a path, without climbing to the **Refugio de Gallegos**. Zigzag down and follow an undulating, rising traverse below cliffs or across steep forested slopes. Zigzag uphill and traverse again, then at a junction, zigzag down to the bouldery bed of **Barranco de Gallegos**.

Cross diagonally upstream to pick up a track, which zigzags steeply uphill, eventually levels out, and roughly traverses along a soft red layer, often wet and dripping. Later, swing right across a slight gap and head steeply downhill, partly on concrete, in a valley in dark, dense laurisilva. The track undulates and reaches a junction. Turn right uphill along a meandering,

Some maps show the route wrongly.

undulating track through laurisilva and pines. Turn left at a junction, straight ahead as marked soon

121

afterwards, and left again soon after that. A three-way signpost is reached at **El Bailadero**, where Walk 29 joins.

Walk straight ahead, but where the track bends sharp right, walk straight ahead down log steps. This is the Camino de los Lances, steep and rugged, in a deep and dark cutting. Emerge at **Los Lances** to walk down a track to a junction, and turn right. A winding red earth track runs down scrub woodland slopes, passing terraces to reach a junction. Walk slightly to the right down a dirt road that broadens, passing three substantial empty buildings. A patchy tarmac road leads down to a junction. ◄

Turn right for Laguna de Barlovento.

Turn left as signposted for Barlovento, round a road bend then sharp right down a track. Turn left as marked at a junction, right later, then left along a concrete road. Cross a main road and follow a narrow, overgrown path, then turn right down a road. Cross the main road again and continue straight ahead down a track. Follow the road to a crossroads where the GR130 crosses (see Walk 41) and continue into **Barlovento** to finish (all services, accommodation, banks with ATMs, post office, shops, bars, buses and taxis).

The Hotel La Palma Romantica lies off-route on the final decent to Barlovento

WALK 24

La Zarza and Don Pedro

Distance	9 or 15km (5½ or 9½ miles)
Start/Finish	Parque Cultural La Zarza
Total Ascent/Descent	400 or 850m (1310 or 2790ft)
Time	2hr 30min or 4hr
Terrain	Rugged, wooded paths, as well as roads and tracks, sometimes steep.
Refreshment	Restaurant off-route at La Mata.
Transport	Buses serve La Zarza from Garafía and Barlovento.

The Parque Cultural La Zarza focuses on the archaeology of La Palma. It also sits in a barranco offering an interesting walk. The lower parts are full of laurisilva forest, and there is an option to link with the GR130, or simply climb back up a forested and cultivated ridge.

Start at the **Parque Cultural La Zarza** and go through a tunnel beneath the road, signposted PR LP 9.2. A broad path runs through laurisilva, passing caves and a rock wall bearing a Guanche carving. The path follows the bed of the barranco to a three-way signpost. Keep right and go down log steps into a dark, wooded gorge where caves are found beneath a dry waterfall. Follow the path along or close to the bed of the **Barranco de Magdalena**, crossing a footbridge. Walk uphill, down log steps, and along a fenced path to the bottom of another dry waterfall. Cross another footbridge and climb along a path, then go down log steps back into the barranco. Cross a footbridge and walk down the bed of the barranco past Fuente de la Caldera del Agua.

The path stays in or close to the bed, usually on the right-hand side. Always go where the markers indicate and climb from the bed as marked up log steps, then

Route uses PR LP 9.2 and GR130.

A footbridge across Caldera de Agua, deep in a gorge full of laurisilva forest

back down log steps to cross it again. After a couple more crossings, the path climbs a steep forested slope, passes a cave full of water, then traverses across a steep slope, past Fuente de la Vica. Emerge at a little plaza at **Cruz del Gallo** and turn left down a road to a three-way signpost. A decision needs to be made, either to extend the route to Don Pedro (see later), or head back up to La Zarza.

Turn right for La Zarza, along a narrow, winding road. Before reaching a house, turn right up a track. Climb past a house and the grassy track becomes quite rugged in laurisilva forest. Two tracks come in from the right, so keep left to keep climbing. After a gentle stretch, at another junction, keep right as marked. There are

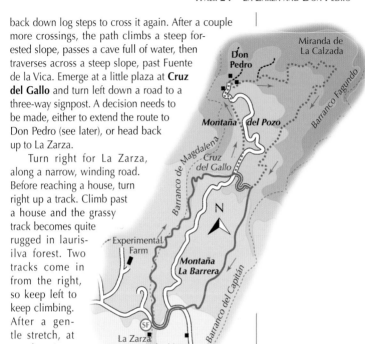

tagasaste bushes on the left, then more laurisilva ahead. Keep right up another track then left up a road. Watch for a marker indicating a right turn down a track, then a left turn up a path. Continue straight ahead up a grassy track, then right up a narrow road, reaching the main road on a bend. Turn right to finish back at **La Zarza**.

Extension to Don Pedro

Walk down the road, signposted PR LP 9.2 for Don Pedro. The road is very bendy, so watch for a path down to the left, and later make a quick short-cut through a bend, then go down a concrete road to houses at **Don Pedro**. Turn sharp right at four odd dragon trees to follow

125

The route can be extended along the GR130 at Don Pedro, before a long climb back to La Zarza

the GR130, or Walk 40. A track runs round and down the slopes of a valley. Walk down a bit of road past a couple of houses, then down steps to follow an easy terrace through heather, onto an open slope. Turn left down a track, pass a house with a dragon tree, then pass a few more houses. Turn right up a concrete road signposted PR LP 9.2 for La Zarza. Follow this as it winds uphill, reaching a house and water-store at the top. Continue up a path as marked, eventually reaching a house, to join the rest of the route to **La Zarza**.

WALK 25

Roque del Faro and Garafía

Distance	15km (9½ miles)
Start	Roque del Faro
Finish	Garafía
Total Ascent	100m (330ft)
Total Descent	750m (2460ft)
Time	4hr
Terrain	Mostly gentle roads, tracks and paths on forested and cultivated slopes, ending with a steep descent.
Refreshment	Bars at Roque del Faro, La Mata and Garafía.
Transport	Buses serve Roque del Faro, La Mata and Garafía from Los Llanos and Barlovento.

This linear route is mostly downhill, starting easily by wandering from Roque del Faro to a restaurant at La Mata. The Parque Cultural La Zarza is passed, which focuses on the archaeology of La Palma. After passing the Ermita de San Antonio, a long track winds down to Garafía.

Start on the main road at a junction beside the Km54 marker at **Roque del Faro**. A PR LP 9 signpost points to Santo Domingo. ▶ Walk along a track and fork left into pine forest and sparse laurisilva. Avoid turnings to properties while turning round little valleys. Cross a road and follow a grassy track, which narrows to a stone-paved path. Cross the rocky bed of **Barranco Carmona** and climb through patchy laurisilva, linking with an overgrown track that becomes stony, passing a few buildings. Turn right downhill, and quickly left, to climb across another track among big pines. Walk down into a little valley and gently uphill. Fork right as signposted, gently downhill and overgrown at times, then a rugged stone-paved path runs through laurisilva. Walk up a track and

Route uses PR LP 9.

'Santo Domingo' is another name for 'Garafía'.

gently down across another, continuing down a path to reach yet another track. Turn left to walk round a valley and climb past a prominent red house.

The track runs onwards and down a bit, where Fuente del Capitán is signposted off-route. Walk up to the main road, crossing to a map-board and bus shelter at **La Mata**, then head for the Restaurante La Mata. The road serving the restaurant ends at a turning space. Follow a track downhill, which narrows to a stone-paved path. Turn left to follow the main road round a bend and go down steps to the **Parque Cultural La Zarza**. ◄

Start of Walk 24.

Walk up the access road and follow the main road up through a cutting. Turn right along a narrow, meandering road to a crossroads. A path is signposted onwards, and a track later runs straight through partly cleared scrub

The church and plaza in the middle of the remote village of Garafía

woodland. An 'experimental farm' nearby is selectively breeding livestock to revive indigenous breeds. Keep walking ahead through a flat recreational area to reach the **Ermita de San Antonio**. This was one of the first areas settled following the Conquest.

Pass the church to find a signpost and follow a dirt road up and down through a deep, crumbling cutting. A bendy track runs down a slope of laurisilva, passing a goat farm and potato plots later, with cistus and rock rose alongside.

There are a couple of ascents, but mostly the track runs downhill and is signposted at junctions, passing houses and clearings. Walk up a tarmac road, climbing round the rugged Barranco de la Luz. A stone-paved road runs steeply downhill, featuring fine stonework divided into 'lanes'. Further down, it gives way to tarmac and links with the GR130 on the edge of **Garafía**. Turn left to walk through the village. (Bank with ATM, post office, shops and bars).

129

WALK 26
Roque del Faro and Franceses

Distance	19km (12 miles)
Start/Finish	Roque del Faro
Total Ascent/Descent	1150m (3770ft)
Time	6hr
Terrain	Steep, forested roads, tracks and paths, as well as steep, rugged paths across a deep barranco.
Refreshment	Bars at Roque del Faro and El Tablado.
Transport	Buses serve Roque del Faro and Franceses from Garafía and Barlovento. A bus occasionally links this service with El Tablado.

The tiny villages of El Tablado and Franceses are perched on either side of the deep and rugged Barranco de los Hombres, while the village of Roque del Faro lies halfway up the highest mountains on La Palma. Amazingly, a circular walk connects all three villages.

Route uses PR LP 9.1 and GR130.

Start at the Bar Restaurante Reyes in **Roque del Faro** and walk down to the main road. Cross over, turn right and

The tiny village of El Tablado and its restaurant on a steep slope

immediately left along a track signposted PR LP 9.1 for El Tablado. There is a gentle rise to an electricity transformer tower, then a steep descent down a grassy, stone-paved track. When a concrete road is reached, turn quickly left and right, then downhill as signposted. Swing right along a gentle grassy track and left down another. Turn left along yet another grassy track and go down a valley in dense laurisilva. Emerge and turn right, passing a small house on a flat bit of land.

Go straight down a grassy path, back into laurisilva, steeply downhill. Emerge with a brief view of a forested crest at **Pico de la Tabaquera**, and swing left through a red pumice gap. Cross a forested valley and climb the other side. Turn a rocky corner and walk downhill, then climb out of the forest to a track on a ridge. Turn right downhill as marked and the track becomes concrete, steepening, then rugged and overgrown. It gives way to a path back into laurisilva, crossing a valley and running level across a steep slope to a road.

Walk down the road, but watch for paths short-cutting bends, particularly on the final descent into the village of **El Tablado**. Pass a bar restaurant, walk down past a church and pass an unmarked shop/bar, reaching a GR130 signpost. Turn right as indicated for Franceses and use the route description at the end of Walk 40 (page 196) to drop into the **Barranco de los Hombres** and climb up the other side.

Mirador El Topo, a viewpoint in the deep Barranco de los Hombres

The road could be followed up to the village of **Franceses**, but after the first bendy stretch, turn right up a path. This zigzags uphill and joins a farm track. Walk along this and keep right at a track junction. Soon afterwards, pass between buildings to reach a road bend.

Turn right to walk round the bend, then turn right again to leave the road, and immediately turn left along a track. Don't turn left to a house, but keep straight ahead along a vegetated path. This becomes more rugged as it climbs, overlooking the **Barranco de las Travesias**.

Climb past cultivation terraces on a well-wooded slope, then continue up through the woods to cross a road on a bend. The path continues climbing, becoming a track that eventually approaches farm buildings. Pass between these and keep right, following a path into the barranco. After winding past wooded and cultivated areas, a track climbs to a road. Turn right to reach a road junction, then left. The road bends around the **Barranco de los Hombres** to return to **Roque del Faro**.

WALK 27

Roque del Faro to Roque de los Muchachos

Distance	12km (7½ miles)
Start	Roque del Faro
Finish	Roque de los Muchachos
Total Ascent	1525m (5005ft)
Total Descent	100m (330ft)
Time	4hr
Terrain	Forest tracks and steep forest paths. Rugged paths on steep and rocky mountains.
Refreshment	Bars at Roque del Faro.
Transport	Buses serve Roque del Faro from Garafía and Barlovento. Walk 28 is the best option for descent.

Most routes that reach Roque de los Muchachos from a bus service are very long and arduous, and are best used as descent routes. The climb from Roque del Faro is admittedly steep, but also fairly short, and can be linked with descents to bus services at Puntagorda or Tijarafe (Walk 28).

Route uses PR LP 9 and GR131.

Start at the Bar Restaurante Reyes in **Roque del Faro**, over 1000m (3280ft), and walk up a road signposted PR LP 9 for Roque de los Muchachos. The road bends right at the Bar Restaurante Roque Faro, but walk straight up a concrete road. Avoid forks to right and left at a goat farm, then turn left as signposted, where a track climbs beside a forest. Follow this among tall pines and swing left, not down a track, but gently up a track. This undulates gently and turns a corner, reaching a junction at a three-way signpost. ◄

La Traviesa, Walk 23, crosses here.

Walk straight ahead and round a left bend, then fork right at a junction. Follow the track past a building, down across a concrete bridge over **Barranco de los Hombres**, to another three-way signpost. Turn right to follow a

narrow path up to a signpost and broader path, then at another signpost follow an old narrow path winding up the forested slope. One stretch runs slightly downhill, otherwise keep climbing and reach a steep crest at **Paso de la Hiedra**, covered in rock rose, broom and bracken.

Cross an old track and climb straight uphill. There are slight breaks of slope, otherwise the ascent is unrelenting. Zigzags ease the gradient for a while then there is another direct climb, before the path becomes grassy and climbs more easily. The pines thin out as the path runs along the left side of a ridge, switching to the right, passing a rocky peak at 1812m (5945ft). Follow the path across a gentle gap among pines, climbing, narrow and stony, on **Moro de la Cebolla**.

The path is clear and outflanks all rocky obstacles, zigzagging first, then traversing the undercut base of a cliff, zigzagging further uphill later. The observatories on Roque de los Muchachos are in view and as the pines give out, masses of broom cover the higher slopes. Watch for a gnarled juniper on a rocky outcrop to the right. The

Cloud crosses the ridge at Moro de la Cebolla as the route emerges from pine forest

135

path is stony, flanked by low walls, zigzagging past **Fuente de la Tamagantera** and a habitable cave. ◄ Zigzags lead up to an orange-coloured track; turn right to follow it gently up to a road and map-board at **Los Andenes**.

There are many hidden 'bivvies' on these mountains.

Turn right down the road to a fine mirador overlooking Caldera de Taburiente, joining the GR131. Leave the road and climb a narrow path, taking care on crumbling ash slopes. Pass through a gap in a wall-like dyke at **Pared de Roberto** and keep climbing. The slopes are bouldery and the path

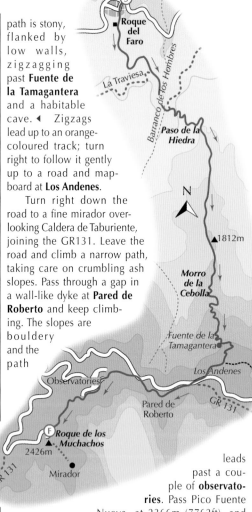

leads past a couple of **observatories**. Pass Pico Fuente Nueva, at 2366m (7762ft), and cross a gap. Climb over a top, passing more observatories. Go down a stony, uneven path to another gap, then cross a rocky hump and follow an easy path

across Degollada del Fraile. Look over the edge to see little shelters.

The path zigzags up to a paved car park and national park kiosk on **Roque de los Muchachos**. Water is often available, and while there is a trig point nearby, the summit rocks rise to 2426m (7959ft), the highest point on La Palma. The rocks are crumbling and access is not permitted. Views stretch across La Palma and across the sea to the islands of El Hierro, La Gomera and El Teide on Tenerife.

It is well worth following a paved path down to a fine viewpoint (**mirador**) overlooking Caldera de Taburiente. If a pick-up cannot be arranged, there are routes available for the descent, the easiest being Walk 28.

Roque de los Muchachos, looking across a 'sea of clouds' filling Caldera de Taburiente

WALK 28

Roque de los Muchachos to Puntagorda or Tijarafe

Distance	17km (10½ miles)
Start	Roque de los Muchachos
Finish	Puntagorda or Tijarafe
Total Ascent	50m (165ft)
Total Descent	1675 or 1825m (5495 or 5990ft)
Time	5hr
Terrain	Gentle, stony paths give way to steeper paths, tracks and roads on forested and cultivated slopes.
Refreshment	Bars at Puntagorda and Tijarafe.
Transport	(Expensive) taxi to start. Buses serve Puntagorda and Tijarafe from Los Llanos, Garafía and Barlovento.

Several old trails converge on the highest mountains, dating from the time when it was easier to cross the mountains than it was to travel round them. A trail running east from Roque de los Muchachos starts at a gentle gradient, then offers a choice of steep descents to Puntagorda, or to Tijarafe by linking with Walk 21.

Route uses PR LP 11 or PR LP 12.

Start from the paved car park on **Roque de los Muchachos**, face the summit rocks, which rise to 2426m (7959ft), keep right of them and turn right down a path to a road. Turn left and walk down past a large metal building. Go round a bend where there is a three-way signpost. The PR LP 11 stays on the road, signposted for Puntagorda and Tijarafe. Don't turn left to the ball-like observatory, but keep ahead down the road on a slope of broom. Turn left at a later junction and pass two mirror dishes, almost reaching helipads at **Tablada del Fraile**. ◄

A path may avoid the road in future.

Turn left as signposted along a broad and stony path through broom, known as the 'Traviesa Alta'. Gradients are gentle and a shallow barranco is crossed. Continue gently down beside a fence, where plots protect uncommon species of broom at **Llano Barona**. The path winds more steeply down a partly forested slope to cross a rocky barranco. Climb and walk across a slope of broom, then cross another sparsely forested barranco. Climb and meander gradually down a stony path, past broom and pines, to a concrete road at **Llano de las Ánimas**. A three-way signpost is reached around 1940m (6365ft). ▸

Walk down the steep road for the PR LP 11 to Puntagorda, watching for yellow/white flashes on the right, heading right as marked from a lay-by. Pick up a narrow path across a water pipe and walk down into pine forest. Stones flank the path, but sometimes it simply runs down a rounded crest. Cross a dirt road and water pipe, and walk down a narrow tarmac road which steepens, with views of vineyards, figs and almonds. Signposts are reached where La Traviesa crosses (see Walk 22).

Keep walking down the road, **Camino de la Rosa**, signposted for Puntagorda, past vines and through forest. Cross a road at a house called Casa Blas and go down a rugged, walled track, which becomes grassy. Enter a

Turn left through a gate for the PR LP 12 to Tijarafe, see later, and a link with Walk 21.

The descent from the mountains, where slopes of broom give way to pine forest

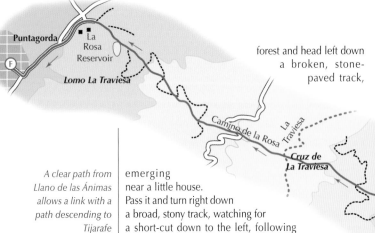

forest and head left down a broken, stone-paved track,

Camino de la Rosa

La Traviesa

Cruz de La Traviesa

A clear path from Llano de las Ánimas allows a link with a path descending to Tijarafe

emerging near a little house. Pass it and turn right down a broad, stony track, watching for a short-cut down to the left, following

a water pipe through a cutting in crumbling ash. Continue along the red track and watch for a signpost on the right for a short-cut down through forest. Cross over the main track, follow an old track, and cross the main track again. Continue down a rugged track and watch carefully as an old grooved path winds down to the main track again.

Keep right of a large **reservoir**, go straight down a short tarmac and concrete track, followed by a forest track, with heather scrub alongside. Cross the main track and continue straight down to a road-end, where the GR130 crosses, close to a campsite at **La Rosa** (see Walk 39). Keep left to follow the road down to a main road. Turn left to reach the Km76 marker and a bus shelter. It is also possible to walk to a nearby junction and go down into **Puntagorda** for a bus (pensión, bank

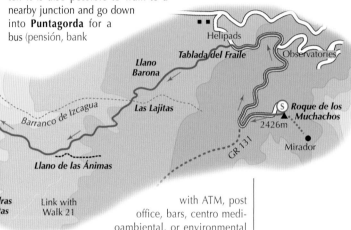

with ATM, post office, bars, centro medioambiental, or environmental centre, and nearby market).

Alternative descent to Tijarafe

At Llano de las Ánimas, turn left through a gate as signposted PR LP 12 for Tijarafe. The fenced area contains a wealth of unusual plants, whose seeds are collected and transplanted elsewhere. Leave through another gate and follow the path down across a gentle barranco. Follow an undulating path and keep right at junctions, crossing a streambed, then another. The next is a little deeper, then pines and broom grow across the slope. After crossing one last streambed, the path rises gently to a three-way signpost at Lomo de las Piedras Altas. Continue straight ahead for Tijarafe and see the last part of Walk 21 for the route description.

WALK 29
Pico de la Cruz to Barlovento

Distance	17km (10½ miles)
Start	Roadside below Pico de la Cruz
Finish	Barlovento
Total Ascent	75m (245ft)
Total Descent	1775m (5825ft)
Time	5hr
Terrain	Rugged paths give way to steep paths on forested slopes, with gentler roads and tracks at the end.
Refreshment	Plenty of choice in Barlovento.
Transport	Taxi to start. Buses serve Barlovento from Santa Cruz and Garafía.

View from Pico de la Cruz, looking southwards towards the Cumbre Vieja

Pico de la Cruz is very easy to climb, mere minutes from the mountain road. A path drops down slopes of broom, followed by steep slopes of pine, then dense, moist laurisilva. It eventually joins a route called La Traviesa, which is followed to Barlovento.

Start high on the mountain road, where there is a map-board at 2280m (7480ft). Climb stone steps to a three-way signpost and turn left to follow the GR131. An easy, dusty, stony path roughly follows a fence, weaving between boulders and broom. The higher of the twin peaks of **Pico de la Cruz** bears a concrete hut at 2351m (7713ft). Enjoy views around La Palma, into the Caldera de Taburiente, and across the sea to the islands of El Hierro, La Gomera and Tenerife. Retrace steps to the road and map-board.

Turn right along the road, then left as signposted PR LP 8 for Barlovento. A stony path, flanked by stones, winds down a stony slope partly covered in broom. The path becomes red and dusty, later boulder-paved. Pines appear and the rugged path winds down past them. A three-way signpost is reached where the PR LP 8 and PR LP 7 branch apart at **Hoyas de las Piedras**, around 1920m (6300ft). This junction is much higher than shown on maps.

Route uses PR LP 8 and PR LP 20.

La Traviesa

El Bailadero

Los Loros

Lomo del Cedro

N

Montaña Alta

Map continues on page 144

Hoyas de las Piedras

Los Dormitorios

S

2351m ▲
Pico de la Cruz

Keep left to follow the PR LP 8 for Barlovento, and this path is obviously more used than the other, dropping, steep and gritty, with a few log steps on a slope of pine and broom. The Barranco de Gallegos falls to the left and rock rose appears among the broom, followed by heather trees

143

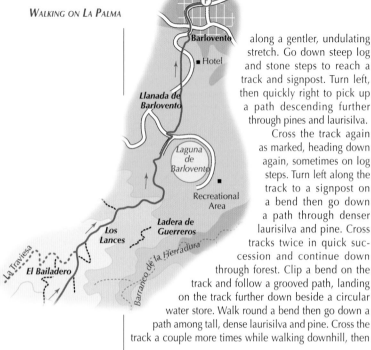

along a gentler, undulating stretch. Go down steep log and stone steps to reach a track and signpost. Turn left, then quickly right to pick up a path descending further through pines and laurisilva.

Cross the track again as marked, heading down again, sometimes on log steps. Turn left along the track to a signpost on a bend then go down a path through denser laurisilva and pine. Cross tracks twice in quick succession and continue down through forest. Clip a bend on the track and follow a grooved path, landing on the track further down beside a circular water store. Walk round a bend then go down a path among tall, dense laurisilva and pine. Cross the track a couple more times while walking downhill, then

The path descends from the road on stony slopes, with a view of Barlovento in the distance

The path is clear and obvious as it enters pine forest

the path becomes rocky and reaches a signpost. Walk along a grassy track, gently down to a junction, and keep straight ahead. Keep straight ahead at another junction to reach a three-way signpost at **El Bailadero**.

Walk 23, La Traviesa, is joined at this point. Turn right to follow it down a path called Camino de los Lances, and refer to the end of Walk 23 for a route description to **Barlovento**.

WALK 30

Pico de la Cruz to Los Sauces or Barlovento

Distance	17 or 19km (10½ or 12 miles)
Start	Roadside below Pico de la Cruz
Finish	Los Sauces
Alternative Finish	Barlovento
Total Ascent	75 or 225m (245 or 740ft)
Total Descent	1985 or 2165m (6510 or 7105ft)
Time	5 or 6hr
Terrain	Rugged paths give way to steep paths on forested slopes, often crossing forest tracks and sometimes overgrown. Roads and tracks at the end are steep.
Refreshment	Plenty of choice in Los Sauces and Barlovento.
Transport	Taxi to start. Buses serve Los Sauces from Santa Cruz and Barlovento.

Pico de la Cruz is very easy to climb, mere minutes from a mountain road. A path drops down slopes of broom, becoming rather overgrown in pine and laurisilva forest. Good tracks are followed later, with options to finish either in Los Sauces or Barlovento.

Route uses PR LP 8 and PR LP 7.

See Walk 29 for the ascent of Pico de la Cruz and the descent to a path junction at Hoyas de las Piedras, where the PR LP 7 and PR LP 8 branch apart. Keep right to follow the PR LP 7 for Los Sauces, which is obviously much less used than the other path. Pine cones, pine needles and broom scrub are awkward at first, but follow the path as it winds downhill. It generally follows a forested crest at an easy gradient, then drops more steeply and becomes overgrown with broom and rock rose. Watch for hidden, crude stone steps, and later broken wooden steps. Reach a forest track and a signpost. ◀

Turning left allows a chance to switch to Walk 29.

The path descends stony, broom-covered slopes, passing a small pine tree

Turn right down the track, and walk down steps from a bend, continuing along another overgrown path. Cross the track further downhill, which is still overgrown, but easier as laurisilva increases among the pines. A long and winding stretch of path eventually lands on the track again. Turn left down it, and it swings right. Stay on it

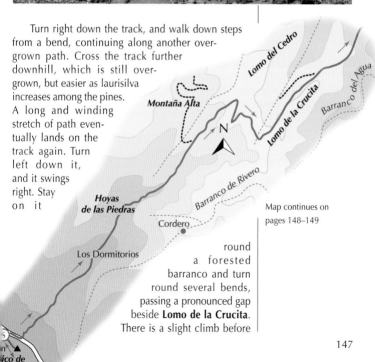

Lomo del Cedro

Lomo de la Crucita

Barranco del Agua

Montaña Alta

N

Barranco de Rivero

Hoyas de las Piedras

Cordero

Map continues on pages 148–149

Los Dormitorios

round a forested barranco and turn round several bends, passing a pronounced gap beside **Lomo de la Crucita**. There is a slight climb before

ico de la Cruz

147

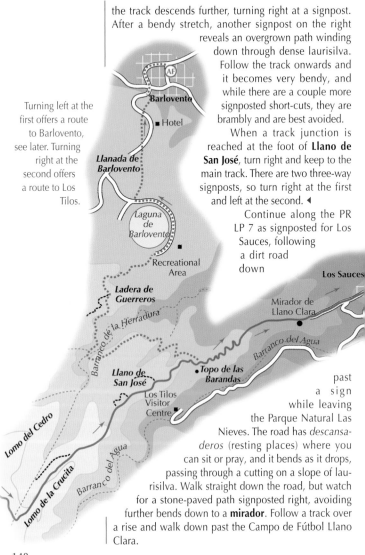

the track descends further, turning right at a signpost. After a bendy stretch, another signpost on the right reveals an overgrown path winding down through dense laurisilva. Follow the track onwards and it becomes very bendy, and while there are a couple more signposted short-cuts, they are brambly and are best avoided.

When a track junction is reached at the foot of **Llano de San José**, turn right and keep to the main track. There are two three-way signposts, so turn right at the first and left at the second. ◀

Continue along the PR LP 7 as signposted for Los Sauces, following a dirt road down

Turning left at the first offers a route to Barlovento, see later. Turning right at the second offers a route to Los Tilos.

past a sign while leaving the Parque Natural Las Nieves. The road has *descansaderos* (resting places) where you can sit or pray, and it bends as it drops, passing through a cutting on a slope of laurisilva. Walk straight down the road, but watch for a stone-paved path signposted right, avoiding further bends down to a **mirador**. Follow a track over a rise and walk down past the Campo de Fútbol Llano Clara.

148

Walk straight downhill by road, on concrete at first, then tarmac, nearly always steep. Watch for the interesting mill, Molino Hidráulico El Regente, dated 1873. A road called La Calle drops through the barrio of La Trasera, passing old houses on the way down to the plaza in the centre of **Los Sauces** (pensión, banks with ATMs, post office, shops, bars, buses and taxis).

Alternative Route to Barlovento

For Barlovento, turn left at the first three-way signpost, to follow the PR LP 7.1, bearing in mind that this is a long option. The track can be muddy, winding in and out of forested barrancos, often flanked by tajinaste and big ferns. Sometimes, the track is cut into a steep slope and sometimes there are views, but usually there is dense

Tall tajinaste growing in forest clearings on the link route to Barlovento

laurisilva forest, deep into the **Barranco de la Herradura**. In the middle of this, and the only place where yellow/white flashes are seen, pass structures associated with water abstraction.

The path climbing out of the barranco has a rustic fence alongside, but parts have collapsed and you should never trust it with your weight. The path undulates, dips to cross a footbridge, then climbs a long flight of log steps, emerging from the forest at a signpost. Walk ahead and the path drops past a few terraces to another signpost, then turn right to follow a track gently downhill. When a shed is reached, turn left down a path, and at the bottom of a wooded slope, turn right up a track. Pass a field and turn right down a concrete track, only as far as a bend, where a signpost hidden in a hedge points straight ahead beside a field. The path becomes rutted as it drops through laurisilva to a road beside the securely fenced reservoir, **Laguna de Barlovento**.

Turning right leads down a concrete road and steep tarmac road to Las Cabezadas.

Turn right to follow the road beside the reservoir, passing a recreational area with cabins, campsite and a restaurant. The whole area is surrounded by laurisilva, with lots of tajinaste growing. The reservoir road approaches an ash cone, but before it there is a three-way signpost. ◄ Keep straight ahead along the road, maybe climbing to miradors on either side.

Follow the road onwards and turn sharp right only when signposted down a track for Barlovento. Turn left as marked at a junction, right later, then left along a concrete road. Cross a main road and follow a narrow, overgrown path, then turn right down a road signposted for Barlovento. Cross the main road again and continue straight ahead down a track. Follow the road to a crossroads where the GR130 crosses (see Walk 41) and continue into **Barlovento** to finish (accommodation, banks with ATMs, post office, shops, bars, buses and taxis).

Church in the centre of Los Sauces, seen from a park-like plaza

WALK 31

Los Sauces and Los Tilos

Distance	10, 16 or 26km (6¼, 10 or 16 miles)
Start	Los Sauces or Casa del Monte
Finish	Los Tilos or Los Sauces
Total Ascent/Descent	350, 500 or 1600m (1150, 1640 or 5250ft)
Time	4hr, 5hr 30mins or 9hr
Terrain	Steep roads, tracks and paths, often rugged and forested. A water channel has to be followed across cliffs and through tunnels.
Refreshment	Plenty of choice in Los Sauces. Bar at Las Lomadas. Bar at Los Tilos.
Transport	Buses serve Los Sauces and Las Lomadas from Barlovento and Santa Cruz. Four-wheel drive taxi to Casa del Monte.

Los Tilos and the Barranco del Agua are clothed in laurisilva forest, with gushing springs at Marcos and Cordero. The water is quickly channelled away down the Lomo de Valle Grande. Taxis are often used to start and finish this route, but a complete circular walk is also possible.

At **Los Sauces**, either hire a four-wheel drive taxi to Casa del Monte, or cross the remarkable bridge, **Puente de Los Tilos**. Turn right into **Las Lomadas**, and climb straight up Calle Verada de Lomadas. Don't turn left as signposted 'Marcos y Cordero', but climb straight up a steep road. Tarmac gives way to steep concrete beyond the last houses, on a slope of wonderfully mixed scrub. Follow a stony track, then another steep stretch of concrete. Climb, steep and stony, past a final building, reaching a signpost on a bend.

Walk round the bend and turn right up a path among laurisilva. Join a track and follow it, forking left. Fork right

Route uses PR LP 6. Option to follow PR LP 7.

151

Be warned – it is very wet in one of the tunnels and full waterproofs will be needed

later up a path with a pipe alongside, up through a cutting, levelling on a crest. Climb again and turn right up a track, and right up a rough concrete track, which may be buried under dirt. Wind up a broad, steep, rugged track, which becomes easier, then climb a deep, narrow, rough-paved groove. The path climbs steeply and intersects four times with bends on a track. Keep climbing as sign-

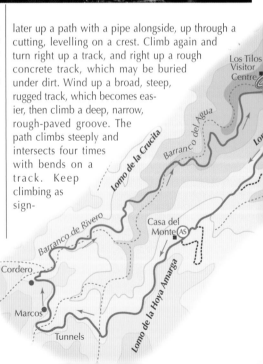

posted and marked, and the path follows a groove on a well-defined ridge. A broad path climbs higher and leads to **Casa del Monte**. Beyond the building is a track and a map-board. ▶ A water channel leads away from the track and the route is unsuitable for anyone with vertigo. The channel runs through laurisilva and is covered as the slope steepens. Reach a tunnel with a gateway and go inside. Slabs have been laid across the channel, headroom diminishes, and the middle is constricted. Emerge and enjoy views, then the next tunnel is short, with good headroom.

This can be reached by four-wheel drive taxi, saving 10km (6 miles) of walking and 1100m (3610ft) of climbing.

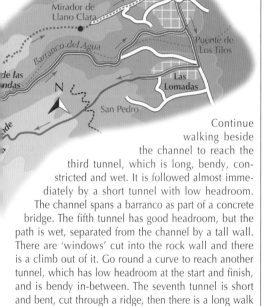

Continue walking beside the channel to reach the third tunnel, which is long, bendy, constricted and wet. It is followed almost immediately by a short tunnel with low headroom. The channel spans a barranco as part of a concrete bridge. The fifth tunnel has good headroom, but the path is wet, separated from the channel by a tall wall. There are 'windows' cut into the rock wall and there is a climb out of it. Go round a curve to reach another tunnel, which has low headroom at the start and finish, and is bendy in-between. The seventh tunnel is short and bent, cut through a ridge, then there is a long walk towards fenced plots where rare plants, *pico de fuego*, are protected.

Go through a short tunnel, then after a short walk, another short tunnel. The path meanders easily beside the channel, dropping below it to pass a water regulator. A viewpoint looks ahead then the tenth tunnel is reached. This has a bit of low headroom and is bent. The next tunnel is short, has low headroom and is bendy, with 'windows' alongside. The twelfth tunnel requires waterproofs to be donned. There is low headroom, constant drips, a vicious side-spout and 'windows' that collect water from cliffs outside, flooding the path.

Leaving the tunnel, the Nacientes de Marcos spout into the channel, while flights of steps climb with wooden and chain fencing alongside. Turn a pronounced corner at the top and follow a bendy stretch of channel. The final tunnel is reached, which has a narrow path inside and some low headroom. Leave it and follow the channel across a slope of pines and tree heather, where the path is easy. More springs, the Nacientes de Cordero, are reached around 1500m (4920ft).

A long and rugged descent leads into the bouldery **Barranco de Rivero**, with zigzags and steep stone steps as the path switches from side to side. Walk down the bed of the barranco until the path is marked for the Centro de Visitantes. Climb a short way and cross a wooden bridge. The path leaves the barranco and climbs past a viewpoint before continuing its descent, where trees limit further views. There are level stretches and lots of steps downhill. Later, cross a wooden bridge over the **Barranco del Agua**.

Climb a path to reach a track then continue up, along and down through dense woodland. The track is hewn from rock and supported by stone buttresses as it zigzags downhill. Eventually it goes through a large and spacious tunnel, emerging to reach a road and car park, around 500m (1640ft). A pick-up or taxi could be arranged here, otherwise turn left or right.

Turning right allows a road-walk down through the barranco. When a road junction is reached at a bridge, turn left to follow a one-way road back to **Los Sauces**, using a generous pedestrian lane.

Turning left allows the road to be followed up to a bar restaurant and a visitor centre at **Los Tilos**. A path climbs above the visitor centre on a steep slope of laurisilva. This

is mostly fenced, includes a couple of short descents, but mostly zigzags up wooden and stone steps. It emerges at the **Mirador del Topo de las Barandas**, overlooking the forested Barranco del Agua. Walk down a track to reach a junction and a three-way signpost. Turn right to follow the PR LP 7 to **Los Sauces**, as described at the end of Walk 30.

Walking deep in the jungle-like barranco on the descent to Los Tilos

WALK 32

Fuente de Olén to Las Lomadas

Distance	19km (12 miles)
Start	Fuente de Olén
Finish	Las Lomadas
Total Ascent	300m (985ft)
Total Descent	1770m (5810ft)
Time	5hr
Terrain	Rugged and sometimes overgrown paths and tracks, ending with a steep forested descent to cultivated slopes.
Refreshment	Bar at Las Lomadas.
Transport	Taxi to start. Buses serve Las Lomadas from Santa Cruz and Barlovento.

This is essentially a *traviesa*, or traverse route. It aims to stay high on slopes of pine forest, connecting a number of trails. Signposts at intervals indicate the PR LP 3, 4 and 5, all descending from the mountains to low-lying villages. The PR LP 6 is used to descend to Las Lomadas.

Route uses PR LP 3.2 and PR LP 6.

Start high on the mountain road, between the Km22 and Km23 markers, at the **Fuente de Olén** recreational area. Take a look at the 17th-century *pozo de la nieve*, or snow-pit. Walk down the road, past the Km22 marker, with a view down the forested **Barranco de Dolores**. A tight left bend is reached where the PR LP 3 (Walk 5) crosses. Turn left as signposted, but keep straight ahead along the PR LP 3.2 for Casa del Monte. A track climbs uphill, flanked by pines and thickets of broom. Walk ahead along a narrow path which looks badly overgrown, but is easily negotiated. Cross a slope of pines and wind down into a forested barranco, walking up the other side to signposts on a forest track near the **Refugio de Puntallana**. Cross

Casa del
Monte

Lomo de la Hoya Amarga

Lomo del Madroñero

Llanos de La Galga

Llano de las Vergas

N

Refugio de
Puntallana

Barranco de Dolores

Fuente
de Olén S

the PR LP 4 (Walk 34),
but follow the track as
signposted PR LP 3.2 for
Casa del Monte.

Map continues on
page 159

Follow the track down
to a bend and turn left down
another track across a little
barranco. Head uphill, a little
overgrown with broom and rock
rose, round a corner to a signpost.
Turn right down a path across
another little barranco, climbing to a four-way signpost.
The PR LP 5 (Walk 33)
crosses here, and
while the PR LP
3.2 is signposted
straight ahead, this
is wrong. Instead,
turn left, then right,
then keep straight
ahead as marked. The
path is overgrown at
Llano de las Vergas, but
passable. Descend more
easily across a little barranco, climb a little then
go down across a rockier
barranco. Climb steeply
among pines then traverse
a rocky, forested slope using
a narrow path. This undulates
among pines and across open
slopes at **Lomo del Madroñero**, broadening to become a
forest track. Keep left at junctions, until the track reaches
a grassy turning space.

Turn right and squeeze through broom and rock rose. The
start of the path isn't easy to spot, and is overgrown in
places, but becomes plainer as it drops, passing a couple of rocky outcrops. As heather and laurisilva develop

157

Crossing a bouldery barranco near Llano de las Vergas

among denser pines, there is less room for scrub. The path drops and winds down **Lomo de la Hoya Amarga** in a groove that becomes quite deep.

Drop onto a track near a map-board beside a water channel, linking with Walk 31, around 1340m (4395ft). ▶

To continue, follow a track towards **Casa del Monte**. Go down a grassy path flashed yellow/white, dropping down a broad, deep, well-wooded cutting. Go down a narrow, winding, grooved path on a well-defined ridge. Drop steeply and intersect four times with bends on a track. Keep walking downhill as signposted and marked. The path is steep, rugged and grooved, sometimes broad and boulder-paved. When it becomes a track and curves markedly left, keep straight ahead downhill. One stretch is concrete although it may be covered in dirt. Go down a narrow, overgrown path with a water pipe alongside. A track continues, then walk down a rugged path to a dirt road and signpost. Just downhill is a junction, so keep left and drop steeply, with a couple of concrete stretches on a wonderfully scrubby slope. A tarmac road drops steeply past the first few houses in **Las Lomadas**. Walk straight down Calle Verada de Lomadas to reach the main road, bar and bus services.

If a four-wheel drive taxi drops anyone here, it could be used to reach Los Sauces.

Casa del Monte, where the route links with Walk 31 to Los Tilos

WALK 33

Fuente Vizcaína to La Galga

Distance	13, 15 or 19km (8, 9½ or 12 miles)
Start	Fuente Vizcaína
Finish	La Galga
Total Ascent	50 or 300m (165 or 985ft)
Total Descent	1750 or 2050m (5740 or 6725ft)
Time	4hr, 4hr 30min or 6hr
Terrain	Awkward, stony and overgrown, then clearer paths and tracks. Options to walk among dense laurisilva or a rugged barranco.
Refreshment	Bars at La Galga.
Transport	Taxi to start. Buses serve La Galga from Santa Cruz and Barlovento.

Starting very awkwardly, this trail slowly gets much better as it descends among pines and laurisilva. The best part comes in a deep, jungle-like valley above La Galga. It is worth dropping below the village, into an arid barranco, then climbing back uphill.

Route uses PR LP 5 and PR LP 5.1.

Start high on the mountain road, around 2100m (6890ft), at the Km28 marker near **Fuente Vizcaína**, where a signpost indicates the PR LP 5 for La Galga. Take careful note of its direction and carefully inch down a slope of rubble. Pass below a rock outcrop, contour and climb slightly, stepping over a less prominent outcrop. Watch for yellow/white flashes, squeezing past broom scrub, keeping well to the right of a small lone pine. Watch for traces of the old path while picking through broom scrub. The path is an overgrown groove, often stony and obscured, but it must be followed faithfully into pine forest, where it becomes easier. Pass a couple of rusty oil drums and note a sudden right turn, reaching a four-way signpost near **Llano de las Vergas**. ▸

Walk 32 crosses here, providing easier access to this route.

Walk ahead as signposted PR LP 5 for La Galga, watching carefully for the path, generally downhill and occasionally along a rocky crest at **Cuesta de Herradores**. The path levels out a couple of times and even climbs slightly, but as the slope steepens, route-finding needs care. Land on a track and turn right to follow it downhill. The track features long and lazy loops, and while short-cuts are signposted, they are badly overgrown, so it makes sense to stay on the track among tall laurisilva. Tajinaste grows alongside from time to time. Follow the track until a three-way signpost is passed, and walk in the direction of La Galga. The track swings to the right, while a grassy track runs straight ahead, and the latter should be followed to the **Mirador de la Somada Alta**. At this point, choose between a rapid descent to La Galga on the PR LP 5, or a longer route via Cubo de La Galga on the PR LP 5.1.

Direct Descent to La Galga
Step left of a rock in front of the mirador and go

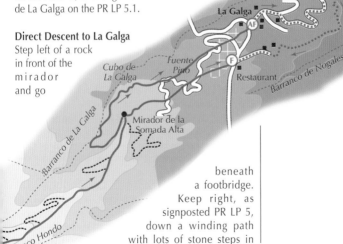

beneath a footbridge. Keep right, as signposted PR LP 5, down a winding path with lots of stone steps in

Deep in jungle-like laurisilva forest in the Barranco de La Galga

dense laurisilva. Reach a house and a concrete road, walk straight ahead down a grassy track, and turn left down a rugged path. Follow this down through a cutting to a house then walk down a concrete road to a cross-roads. Walk straight ahead down a tarmac road, through a crossroads at **Fuente Pino**, to continue down the steep and narrow Calle Fuente Pino. Reach the main road in **La Galga** near the Restaurante Casa Asterio.

Descent via Cubo de La Galga

Leave the mirador as signposted PR LP 5.1 for Cubo de La Galga, down a winding track into the **Barranco de La Galga**, which is full of tall laurisilva. Turn right to follow a path down to the bouldery bed of the barranco. Later, the bed is lost to view in a deep, dark gorge and the path is fenced, rising and falling, muddy along one stretch. A three-way signpost is reached, so walk ahead and climb as the path clings to a steep, forested slope. It later runs down beside a water pipe to a concrete road and map-board. Follow the concrete road and a bendy tarmac road downhill to a signpost. Turn left down a narrow, stone-paved path and straight ahead along a concrete road. Go down past a few houses, cross a road and climb a few steps to short-cut a bend. Cross a road and walk down a concrete road, passing under the other road. Cross the road again and walk down the concrete Calle Llano Molino, reaching the main road at a crossroads at **La Galga**.

Extension below La Galga

To extend the walk, cross the main road and follow Calle San Bartolome to a little church and bar. Turn right behind the church and left down a road. ▶ Turn right later and tarmac gives way to concrete, passing a bakery. Walk down the concrete road, across the scrubby slopes of an ash cone, then turn sharp left down past vines, round and

A fenced path crosses wonderfully scrubby, rocky slopes in the Barranco de Nogales

down through a valley. Don't take the first concrete road down to the right, but take the second, down to a concrete hut. Go past it, towards the sea, to find a three-way signpost where the GR130 crosses (see Walk 42.)

Turn right to follow a fenced path past bananas, dipping in and out of a scrubby, stony little valley. Turn right up a concrete road to pass a banana tent, and turn left down a fenced path, zigzagging down to another three-way signpost in the **Barranco de Nogales**. Turn right to follow the PR LP 5 for La Galga, up a narrow path across a scrubby slope, mostly on crunchy red ash. Sometimes the path is merely a nick in the slope, with fine views of the barranco, but unsuitable for vertigo sufferers. The ash changes from red to black and after turning a corner, caves can be seen hacked into a cliff.

Turn another corner to walk carefully through a brambly side-valley. Climb past a curious stump of rock to find a signpost and turn left along an earth track, which changes to concrete, climbing past houses as the Calle Cercado Peñón. Reach the main road in **La Galga** near the Restaurante Casa Asterio.

Caves with doors, cut into soft volcanic ash in the Barranco de Nogales

WALK 34

Pico de la Nieve to Puntallana or Tenagua

Distance	16 or 22km (10 or 13¾ miles)
Start	Mountain road between Km24 and Km25
Finish	Puntallana
Alternative Finish	La Lomadita, Tenagua
Total Ascent	35 or 375m (115 or 1230ft)
Total Descent	1535 or 1910m (5035 or 6265ft)
Time	4hr 30min or 7hr
Terrain	Optional mountain climb. Long, winding forest tracks and paths, sometimes steep or overgrown, ending on cultivated slopes.
Refreshment	Bars at Puntallana and near Tenagua.
Transport	Taxi to start. Buses serve Puntallana and La Lomadita from Santa Cruz and Barlovento.

Pico de la Nieve can either be climbed or omitted at the start of this walk. The descent runs through pine and laurisilva forest, splitting to offer two finishing points. The clearest route drops to Puntallana, while a less clear alternative route drops to Tenagua.

To climb **Pico de la Nieve**, see Walk 5, and return to the road to continue. Walk past the Km25 marker to a junction with a forest road at a sign for the Parque Natural Las Nieves. Walk down the forest road as signposted PR LP 4 for Puntallana. The road swings sharply right, then a path is flashed yellow/white to the left. It descends easily, cutting a bend from the track and crossing it further down. Continue down the slope, turning right along a ridge, and down to the track again. Turn right down the track, and after a few bends, turn right as marked down a path, short-cutting a bend. There are two three-way signposts close together, where Walk 32 crosses. Follow the PR LP 4 for Puntallana, gently down to the **Refugio de Puntallana**.

Route uses PR LP 4 and PR LP 4.1.

View southwards from the summit of Pico de la Nieve to the Cumbre Vieja

Walk ahead and the path drops, steep and gritty, reaching the track again further downhill. Turn left round a bend and right down a path, and repeat the same procedure lower down the track. The path becomes steep, worn, gritty and slippery on the way down to another

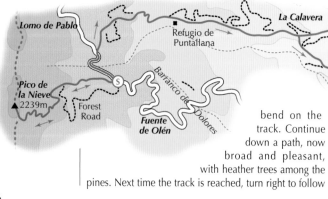

bend on the track. Continue down a path, now broad and pleasant, with heather trees among the pines. Next time the track is reached, turn right to follow it to a three-way signpost, around 1450m (4760ft), at **La Calavera**. This is where the route splits for Puntallana or Tenagua. ▶

The junction is much higher than shown on some maps.

Descent to Puntallana

Follow the PR LP 4 for Puntallana. Walk down a path through pines and laurisilva, crossing the track again at a bend. The narrow and vegetated path broadens as it drops through a cutting, passing stout pines. Land on a track at a signpost and fork right (not **turn** right) up a narrow path that isn't particularly well marked. Walk down through a cutting and cross the track again. Walk further downhill and reach the track yet again at a three-way signpost at **Las Moraditas**.

Keep straight ahead down a path, short-cut a bend, quickly crossing the track again. Go down through a cutting, along a level, brambly crest, and down through another cutting. The path bends left, but watch for a right turn through a deep cutting, down among tall laurisilva. Cross an overgrown track a couple of times, following a long, narrow, winding, grooved path worn down to slippery bedrock. A track and water pipe are reached, so cross the track, step up over the pipe, and follow pipes down through a cutting to pass a waterworks building.

Walk straight ahead down a track, and straight ahead down

from a junction, following a red dirt road. When another junction is reached, Pista El Granel is left and Pista del Cementerio is right, and the latter is also signposted for Puntallana. Walk down the track to a concrete water building where tracks split. Keep left, then immediately right down a path on the slopes of **Zamagallo**. Follow a pipe through a deep cutting and follow a track down from a covered reservoir. Go down to the left through deep and narrow cuttings in crumbling ash beds, squeezing through the undergrowth. Pass a cave and later watch for a left turn, continuing down through the overgrown cutting. Walk down a red earth path to a concrete crossroads, and go straight ahead along the only road running downhill. Keep straight ahead along a tarmac road, down to the main road on the outskirts of **Puntallana**.

Descent to Tenagua

Parts of this route are shown incorrectly on some maps.

Follow the PR LP 4.1 for Tenagua. Walk down a steep and narrow path on a slope of pines and laurisilva. Reach a bend on a track where there are marker posts, and go down a rather overgrown winding path. Look for evidence of use, sawn-off branches and occasional

A stone-paved track running down through laurisilva on the way to Tenagua

yellow/white flashes. There is a slight rise, then a broader path winds downhill. Reach an old track and a four-way signpost near **Lomo del Corcho**. Walk straight ahead down a grassy old track for Tenagua, which gives way to a narrow, winding, steepening path dropping to a very vegetated old track. Turn right to follow this roughly level, and when it is blocked, turn left over an earth bank to continue down a path. Watch carefully on a small, level, overgrown patch, for a yellow/white flash on a stout pine, which is easily missed.

The path runs along a crest and down a groove, along and down again, and yet again. Drop onto a broader path, winding on a slope of laurisilva, landing on a track at a four-way signpost. Keep straight ahead for Tenagua down crumbling steps cut into ash and pumice. The path often has a pipe alongside as it runs down through laurisilva. A forested peak is seen ahead across a gap, and the path rises towards it, heading right across its slopes, high above **Barranco Seco**. The path drops, steep, rocky, gritty and slippery, ending with chunky stone steps down to a gap. Climb along a crest of laurisilva then the path heads right and is cut into rock. A gentle descent leads to a track.

Follow the track uphill a little, then down, and always keep straight ahead as marked and signposted. Step to the left as indicated by a marker post, down a clear path among pines and cistus scrub. Keep straight ahead down a track with a pipe alongside, until a signpost for Tenagua reveals a terrace path to the right at **Llano de Tenagua**. This is overgrown, but look ahead to farm buildings and head left of them.

Turn left down a concrete road and walk straight downhill as marked. Go down a rugged red earth track and fork left as marked down a path. Don't follow a narrow path through scrub, but follow a boulder-paved path with low walls and a pipe alongside. This becomes narrow and overgrown, but is passable. Go straight down a walled, concrete track and turn left along a concrete road. Turn right steeply downhill and right again to reach the main road and a bus shelter at **La Lomadita**.

WALK 35

GR130: Santa Cruz de La Palma to Mazo

Distance	14km (8¾ miles)
Start	Santa Cruz
Finish	Villa de Mazo
Total Ascent	700m (2295ft)
Total Descent	100m (330ft)
Time	4hr
Terrain	Mostly roads and tracks, with linking paths, on steep urban, cultivated and occasionally forested slopes.
Refreshment	Plenty of choice in Santa Cruz, Breña Alta and Mazo.
Transport	Buses serve Breña Alta and Mazo from Santa Cruz, Fuencaliente and Los Llanos.

The GR130, Camino de la Costa, encircles La Palma. It can be started and finished anywhere and walked in either direction. It is presented here in eight daily stages, clockwise. This stage runs from Santa Cruz to Mazo, with steep urban slopes giving way to terraced cultivated slopes.

Leave the Plaza de España in **Santa Cruz**, climbing steps beside the church, turning left and right up Calle San Sebastián, through the Plaza San Sebastián. Climb a steep road to a cobbled plaza at Cajita Blanca, then climb a steep, cobbled road, turning left to a tarmac road. Cross over and turn left up a narrow road, signposted GR130 and PR LP 1. Walk up Calle Calsinas and cross the main road near a shop. Climb past another shop to cross the main road, then go up a short cobbled road to reach a building marked 'Aguas Potables'.

Turn left up the main road, right up a steep road, later passing a bend on the main road. Continue up the steep Calle La Cuesta, cross the main road and follow a road up past Cruz de Las Animas. Pass a bus stop on a bend on the

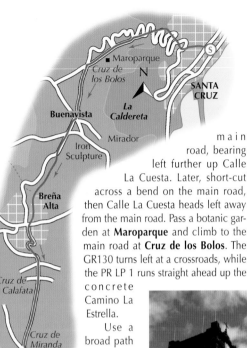

Map continues on
page 172

m a i n
road, bearing
left further up Calle
La Cuesta. Later, short-cut
across a bend on the main road,
then Calle La Cuesta heads left away
from the main road. Pass a botanic garden at **Maroparque** and climb to the
main road at **Cruz de los Bolos**. The
GR130 turns left at a crossroads, while
the PR LP 1 runs straight ahead up the

*GR130 can be started
on the Plaza d'España
in the centre of Santa
Cruz*

c o n c r e t e
Camino La
Estrella.

Use a
broad path
beside the
road to a
roundabout
at Cruce de La
Glorieta. Walk straight past
an **iron sculpture** straddling
the road. The route is flashed
red/white along the narrow
Camino Real, left of and parallel to the main road. Walk
down it and climb Calle Blas
Perez Gonzalez, then walk
down Calle del Cura, passing below the church of San
Pedro in **Breña Alta** (banks
with ATMs, post office, shops,
bars, restaurants, buses and
taxis).

171

Cross the main road and follow Calle Luis Wandevalle a short way, then go down the concrete Calle Cuesta la Pata, and turn right down the concrete Camino la Herradura, which becomes stone-paved. Turn left down a road, then either right uphill at a junction, or short-cut as marked through scrub. Follow a road uphill, noting an old gateway to the left. Further up, Cruz del Rosal is on the right, quickly followed by Cruz de la Plaza. Climb further to **Cruz de la Calafata**, on the right, and another old gateway on the left. Keep climbing ahead, with another old gateway on the right. Pass **Cruz de Miranda** ◀ and walk straight uphill. Almost reach a main road, but walk parallel as flashed red/white along a narrow road.

Cross the main road and follow a road at a higher level (Walk 8 crosses here). Walk down a concrete road, marked for Mazo, crossing Barranco de Amargasinos. Walk up and down to join a road, turning quickly left, right and left to continue up to Cruz de las Breveritas. Turn right as signposted up a road, then up a short concrete and stone-paved track on the right. A short path leads back to the road, then on the left, a concrete road climbs past **Montaña de la Breña**. The GR130 coincides with the PR LP 18.1 (Walk 8) for a while.

Climb the concrete road with woodland to the left and a curious building to the right. Follow an ash path to a road junction and go straight down the road past a forested recreational area. Go up and along the road, past **Cruz de la Rosa** and the ruined Casa del Tabac. Pass Cruz del Pecado and Cruz del Monte then head downhill. Fork right up a road signposted for Mazo. This becomes a fine country track, stone-paved and grassy, climbing gradually across cultivated slopes at the back of a small cone. Reach a complex road junction and mapboard at **Poleal** where Walk 9 crosses.

Walk along the road signposted for Mazo, down and up to another cross at a crossroads. Continue straight along a track, Camino las Toscas, across the slopes of Montaña las Toscas, where there is a recreational area. Walk down the road to a signpost

All these wayside crosses are decorated on 3 May, celebrating the discovery of the True Cross in AD325.

*Fertile volcanic soil
is put to the plough
above La Rosa*

where Walk 10 crosses. Either keep straight ahead along
the GR130, or turn left down to **Mazo** (bank with ATM,
post office, shops, bars, buses, agricultural and craft
markets).

WALK 36
GR130: Mazo to Fuencaliente

Distance	19km (12 miles)
Start	Villa de Mazo
Finish	Fuencaliente
Total Ascent	500m (1640ft)
Total Descent	300m (985ft)
Time	5hr
Terrain	Mostly gentle roads and tracks. Some linking paths are overgrown or rugged. Cultivated and scrubby slopes give way to forest.
Refreshment	Bars at Tirimaga, Tigalate, Montes de la Luna and Fuencaliente.
Transport	Buses serve Mazo, Tirimaga, Tigalate, Montes de la Luna and Fuencaliente from Santa Cruz and Los Llanos.

The GR130 spends all day climbing gradually from Mazo, across cultivated and scrub-covered slopes, onto forested lava flows. Three small villages along the way each offer a bar and bus services. A short descent on the GR131 leads to Fuencaliente.

Start on the main road in **Mazo** and climb steeply as signposted PR LP 16. Reach a three-way signpost close to a recreational area at **Montaña las Toscas**. Turn left to pick up the GR130, walking up a road, over a rise, ahead and gently down to the end of the Camino las Toscas. Keep straight ahead downhill at a junction, and when the main road is seen round a left bend, turn right along a vague track signposted GR130, keeping right of a concrete reservoir. Cross a road and continue straight along a path that becomes a track, passing crosses at **El Calvario**.

Climb parallel to the main road, bearing left onto a narrow, overgrown path, wonderfully flowery, with heather trees and tabaibal. Cross a concrete track and go straight up through a crossroads. Turn left as marked and signposted up a rocky path, reaching a road-end and wayside cross at **Los Cavaderos**. Go up and along the road, which broadens, passing a signpost for the PR LP 16.1 (Walk 10). Keep straight ahead, and the road is noisy with barking dogs, all tethered. Walk down past overgrown plots, where fig trees are lost among heather trees, prickly pears and rampant scrub. Almost reach the main road at a junction near **Tirimaga** (shop/bar off-route).

Turn right up a narrow path, past agaves, heather trees and prickly pears. This quickly becomes an overgrown, walled track, the old highway, dropping to the main road. Turn right by road, past a ruin and cross **Barranco de la Lava**. Walk towards another ruin, but **don't** fork left down a track as marked, as it is awkward to get back onto the road. Instead, stay on the road until a signpost points up to the right. The path looks overgrown, but is fairly easy to follow parallel to the road, past flowery scrub, tabaibal and heather trees. Join and follow the road a short way to cross **Barranco de la Reja** and turn left, then quickly right, to follow another overgrown path below the road. Walk up a stone-paved path to a junction of the main road and Camino Tiguerorte. Turn left towards a bus stop, but right before it to pass signposts and pick up a path rising beside a barranco. ▶

Map continues on page 176

Stay on the road if you want to visit Tigalate, which has a shop and bar.

A stone-paved path climbs beside the barranco, giving way to a track or road, passing a PR LP 15 signpost (Walk 12). Drop down to a road junction and turn right, more or less level above **Tigalate**, then gradually downhill. The tarmac ends abruptly, so continue along a grassy terrace and pass in front of a white-walled cemetery, along and down another terrace. Follow a narrow road down from a house, but watch for a grassy track up to the right later. A path continues and drops into the rugged **Barranco del Cabrito**,

175

which is spanned by a water pipe. Make a left turn to follow a stone-paved track and pipe uphill, pass a few houses and walk mostly on tarmac to the main road at **Barranco Mederos**. Turn right to follow the road across **Barranco de los Palitos Blancos**, watching for a red/white flash beside a house on the right. ◄

Climb a steep, stone-paved or rocky path

Stay on the road if you want to visit Montes de la Luna, which has a shop and two bars.

Piño de la Virgen

GR 131

GR 130

Fuencaliente

F

A track has been cut across lava flows above Montes de la Luna

alongside the barranco, towards pine forest. Turn left when a signpost is reached and follow a winding, undulating track across a slope partly planted with vines. Head downhill and keep left at a

junction, eventually reaching a road and signpost above **Montes de la Luna**. Turn right uphill and a signpost points right up a stone-paved path. Cross black ash or awkward stones, on slopes of scrub and pines. The path undulates across a lava flow from the 1646 eruption of Volcán Martín. Avoid paths down to the road or uphill, and keep straight ahead along an ash track on slopes of pine. Pass the huge **Pino de La Virgen** and turn right at a track junction (left leads to the main road).

The track climbs gradually from the forest across scrubby slopes bearing small vineyards. Reach a signposted junction where the GR130 crosses the GR131. Turn left down the GR131 (referring to Walk 45) to **Fuencaliente** (accommodation, bank with ATM, post office, shops, bars, buses and taxis).

WALK 37
GR130: Fuencaliente to Los Llanos

Distance	27km (17 miles)
Start	Fuencaliente
Finish	Los Llanos de Aridane
Total Ascent	350m (1150ft)
Total Descent	700m (2300ft)
Time	7hr
Terrain	Forest tracks and rugged paths cross lava flows, giving way to road-walking.
Refreshment	Bars at Jedey, San Nicolás, Triana and Los Llanos.
Transport	Buses serve Fuencaliente, Jedey and San Nicolás from Los Llanos and Santa Cruz.

Forested slopes give way to rugged lava that dates only from 1949 on the way to Jedey and San Nicolás. A long road-walk continues to Los Llanos, through well-settled and cultivated countryside. The

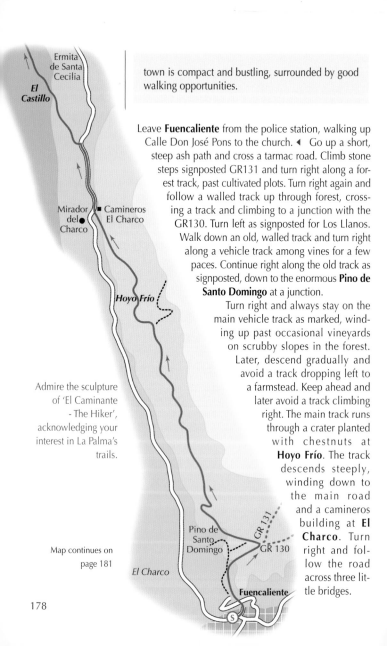

El Castillo

Ermita de Santa Cecilia

Mirador del Charco • ■ Camineros El Charco

Hoyo Frío

Admire the sculpture of 'El Caminante - The Hiker', acknowledging your interest in La Palma's trails.

Map continues on page 181

Pino de Santo Domingo

El Charco

GR 131
GR 130

Fuencaliente
S

town is compact and bustling, surrounded by good walking opportunities.

Leave **Fuencaliente** from the police station, walking up Calle Don José Pons to the church. ◄ Go up a short, steep ash path and cross a tarmac road. Climb stone steps signposted GR131 and turn right along a forest track, past cultivated plots. Turn right again and follow a walled track up through forest, crossing a track and climbing to a junction with the GR130. Turn left as signposted for Los Llanos. Walk down an old, walled track and turn right along a vehicle track among vines for a few paces. Continue right along the old track as signposted, down to the enormous **Pino de Santo Domingo** at a junction.

Turn right and always stay on the main vehicle track as marked, winding up past occasional vineyards on scrubby slopes in the forest. Later, descend gradually and avoid a track dropping left to a farmstead. Keep ahead and later avoid a track climbing right. The main track runs through a crater planted with chestnuts at **Hoyo Frío**. The track descends steeply, winding down to the main road and a camineros building at **El Charco**. Turn right and follow the road across three little bridges.

Watch for a yellow/white flashed track dropping to the left. This descends steeply at times, winding across bouldery forested slopes. Keep left at an intersection of tracks, as signposted for Los Llanos. Emerge from the forest on rugged lava flows, with patches of greenery in-between, while the **Ermita de Santa Cecilia** is high above. Cross a couple of tongues of lava and then drop towards a tiny derelict farmstead.

Keep right to climb above it, passing almonds, figs, prickly pears and a few stout pines. Cross a broader lava flow and keep right of a goat pen. Walk up and straight ahead as marked, avoiding a concrete track, climbing towards the main road, passing another ruined farmstead. Drop a little then climb a few steps, and follow a winding path through a vegetated area. Later, the path is hammered out of a broad lava flow, undulating and crossing another vegetated area. Climb an ash path at the **Malpais de la Cruz Alta** and watch for markers, turning right up a track and left as signposted near houses. Reach the main road beside an ash cone and walk straight through **Jedey** (pizzeria, shop and bar).

A track has been cut across lava flows below the Ermita de Santa Cecilia

The old highway of Camino Campitos has undergone restoration work

Follow the main road past lots of vineyards and watch for the Km39 marker, where Walk 13 comes in from the right. Head left down the Camino Tamanca, below the main road. Keep right at a junction and watch for a path climbing back to the main road at a wayside shrine at Km40. Follow the main road to **San Nicolás** (shops, bars and buses) and out the other side, down through a cutting in black lava. Pass the turning for Todoque, and shortly afterwards, turn right onto the forecourt of a building. Follow a path round the back to reach a road junction. Walk straight ahead down the road, parallel to the main road, until both join.

Cross the main road to a picnic site under eucalyptus trees. Follow the newly stone-paved Camino Campitos down past a 17th-century gateway, Portada Montaña Cogote. The rest is a dirt road, plain and obvious down through **Los Campitos**, straight ahead through a crossroads. Old terraces are dotted with buildings old and new. The road becomes tarmac and continues downhill, passing junctions around **El Pedregal**, many with wayside crosses. Go through a crossroads at **Cruz Chica**, where there is a shop, and continue straight down Camino Nicolás Brito Pais. The road rises and falls, then watch for a right turn at a junction along Camino los Fuentes.

Next, near **Las Martelas**, watch for a narrow path signposted for Los Llanos, between banana tents. This becomes a track, then a concrete road, then continue along a tarmac road, Camino Malpais de Triana. Pass a junction and go under a new road bridge. Reach a junction with Camino de Triana and turn left, now in tandem with Walk 6 as far as a little plaza at **Triana**. Turn right along Calle Pedro Miguel Hernandez Camacho, passing a café and shop on the way towards **Los Llanos**. To get through

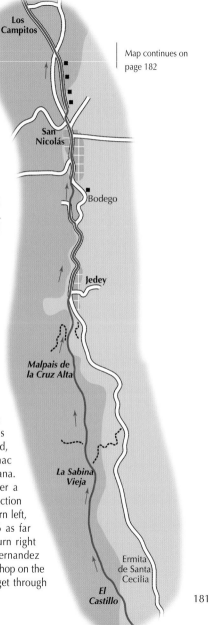

Map continues on page 182

181

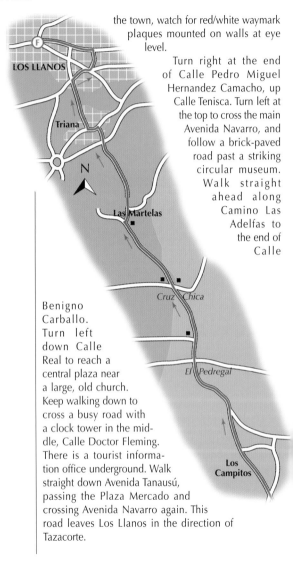

the town, watch for red/white waymark plaques mounted on walls at eye level.

Turn right at the end of Calle Pedro Miguel Hernandez Camacho, up Calle Tenisca. Turn left at the top to cross the main Avenida Navarro, and follow a brick-paved road past a striking circular museum. Walk straight ahead along Camino Las Adelfas to the end of Calle Benigno Carballo. Turn left down Calle Real to reach a central plaza near a large, old church. Keep walking down to cross a busy road with a clock tower in the middle, Calle Doctor Fleming. There is a tourist information office underground. Walk straight down Avenida Tanausú, passing the Plaza Mercado and crossing Avenida Navarro again. This road leaves Los Llanos in the direction of Tazacorte.

WALK 38
GR130: Los Llanos to Puntagorda

Distance	25km (15½ miles)
Start	Los Llanos de Aridane
Finish	Puntagorda
Total Ascent	1400m (4595ft)
Total Descent	1000m (3280ft)
Time	7hr 30min
Terrain	A fiddly succession of roads, tracks and paths, often through settled rural areas, sometimes crossing steep and rugged barrancos.
Refreshment	Bars at La Punta, Tijarafe, Tinizara and Puntagorda.
Transport	Buses serve Tijarafe, Tinizara, El Roque and Puntagorda from Los Llanos and Garafía.

As the GR130 runs northwards, it crosses a few deep and rugged barrancos, starting with the enormous Barranco de las Angustias. The rather fiddly route runs through Tijarafe and Tinizara to reach Puntagorda, crossing and re-crossing the main road.

Leave **Los Llanos** along the Avenida Navarro, as if for Tazacorte. Pass the Palacio del Vino and a plaza in **Argual**, then a water sculpture. When the main road later bends left, keep right of the Plaza de José Ma Hernadez Ramos. Walk along Calle Velazquez, turning left, then left again down Calle Vázquez Díaz. Walk down Camino Punta de Argual on a steep, scrubby slope. After the road makes a sharp right, turn sharp left down the cobbled Camino las Angustias.

Cross the main road at the Km101 marker and go down a steep, stony path and track on a scrubby slope. Cross the road again and walk down a steep concrete and cobbled track past bananas. Turn right and walk down the road from the Km100 marker, passing a large gap then turning left through a small gap in the roadside barrier. A cobbled path winds down between bananas. Cross a footbridge and cross the road on the valley floor, then start climbing beneath overhanging boulder beds.

The path is paved and fenced at first, winding up to the main road. Cross and keep climbing up a scrubby slope, and cross the road again. The path is slightly to the right up steps, then parallel to the road. Turn left along a track before the Km97 marker and rise gently between banana tents. Climb a very steep concrete road past bananas, go up stone steps, and zigzag up a stone-paved path on steep, scrubby slopes. Cross a pipeline then cross the main road, heading slightly right to pick up the stone-paved path. Climb **Laderas de Amagar** to a gap where the path ducks beneath water pipes, reaching a signposted intersection with the GR131 (Walk 43), around 610m (2000ft).

Continue straight ahead as signposted GR130 for Tijarafe along a stone-paved path, with a view of well-settled, cultivated and scrubby slopes, with forest above. Walk ahead and down a track, crossing the main road at the Km92 marker and a bus shelter at **La Punta**. Walk down between a shop and a bar, turning right to a junction. Walk straight up a road and just before the main road, turn left down a narrow path. Cross old terraces, winding in and out of valleys. Cross a concrete road and drop into a valley to follow a track. Turn right uphill as marked to another track, then watch for a path on the left, climbing round a valley of agaves. Climb a concrete road but watch for a grassy path on the left. Pass

Map continues on page 186

Barranco de las Gomeros

GR131

La Punta

GR131

Laderas de Amagar

GR131

El Time

Barranco de las Angustias

La Vera

LOS LLANOS

Argual

S

A zigzag path climbs steeply above the Barranco de las Angustias

a few small buildings and follow a farm road up to the main road.

Cross the main road and walk up a road, forking left up a concrete drive and quickly left up a rugged path. Join a road and follow it up from a concrete water store. Watch for a stone-paved path down to the left, along an almond terrace above the main road. Drop onto a track and turn right into **Barranco de los Gomeros**, then sharp left up a narrow path perched directly above the road. Turn right at a house and follow its access road up and then down. Turn right at a junction, along and down a track to Casa Tia Rosario. A path runs down to a recreational area at **Fuente del Toro**.

Cross the main road and follow a path parallel, down into a barranco and up the other side. Climb steps onto a paved plaza. Don't follow the main road, but look for a path dropping from it, which links with a concrete road into a valley. A path on the right climbs to a chapel at **El Jesús**. Just below is a signpost for Tijarafe, where Walk 20 joins.

Map continues on page 188

A stone-paved path on slopes of tabaibal drops into the Monumento Natural **Barranco del Jurado**, crossing a rocky gap before the lush green bed of the barranco is reached. Walk down it and duck under a pipe, then turn right into the bed of another barranco. Turn right up the bed, turn left later, then zigzag up to the main road and cross it. Zigzag higher and level out, then turn right and quickly left on a road to find a path dropping to the main road. Turn right up it and right again up a quiet block-paved road, reaching a plaza and church in **Tijarafe** (bank with ATM, post office, shops, bars, buses and taxis).

Turn right up a cobbled path and go behind the church, then down to the main road to follow it in the direction of Puntagorda. Go round a bend and turn left along Calle Acceso al Colegio, passing a college and a shop. Follow the road ahead and downhill, branching right down a track signposted for

Barranco de la Baranda

Barranco del Pinillo

Barranco de la Cueva Grande

N

Tijarafe

Barranco del Jurado

El Jesús

Fuente del Toro

Barranco de las Gomeros

Puntagorda, past almonds. Turn left down a stone-paved track to reach a road. Turn right down the road, passing exotic scrub, palms and almonds in a valley. Turn right as signposted up a steep, stone-paved path, cross a road and follow a terrace path. Swing into **Barranco de la Cueva Grande** and climb a stone-paved path, turning left down a quiet tarmac road.

Turn right along a concrete road that drops, climbs steeply, then runs ahead. Keep right and walk down a track towards a cave house. Turn left down a path, crossing rugged **Barranco del Pinillo**, full of almonds, agaves and dense scrub. Follow a terrace path to a road then watch for signposts and markers. The route keeps switching between winding roads and winding paths, over and over, until eventually a path climbs across a road and

Crossing the Barranco del Jurado between El Jesús and Tijarafe

187

drops into the rugged **Barranco de la Baranda**. Zigzag and climb a steep, paved path between almonds and palms. Cross a road, cutting a bend from it, and walk up the road through **Tinizara** (bars and a shop).

Cross the main road to continue as signposted for Puntagorda, passing houses and almonds. Turn left down a road a short way, then right along a track as marked. Climb steeply, but before the top, step left along a narrow terrace. This leads among pines and rock rose, zigzagging down into **Barranco de Garome**. Walk down the bouldery bed but watch for a path leaving it, climbing well above the main road, with pines and rock rose giving way to almonds. Cross a road, Carretera de Montaña, and follow a gentle grassy track and a concrete track down to the main road.

Go down the road a little and turn left as signposted for Puntagorda. Walk down a concrete track, Camino Real Roque, and continue down a grassy, stone-paved track around **Barranco del Roque** and up the other side. Turn quickly right and left up a concrete track, leaving it on the left to go down a track that is grassy, stone-paved, concrete and tarmac in quick succession. Aim for the main road, but turn left just before it through **El Roque**.

Turn left down the main road, cross over at a little shop, and continue along a narrow road signposted for Puntagorda. This rises and falls, then cross the main road and head down to the left of the Vialpa building. Watch for a right turn down a grassy path passing almonds. Reach a steep road, which the GR130 crosses, but if visiting **Puntagorda**, turn left down the road (pensión, bank with ATM, post office, bars, Centro Medioambiental (environmental centre) and nearby mercadillo, or market).

WALK 39

GR130: Puntagorda to Garafía

Distance	17km (10½ miles)
Start	Puntagorda
Finish	Garafía
Total Ascent	400m (1310ft)
Total Descent	780m (2560ft)
Time	4hr
Terrain	Mostly good paths and tracks, but sometimes steep and rugged across barrancos, ending with a road-walk.
Refreshment	Bars or cafés off-route at Las Tricias and Buracas. Bars at Garafía.
Transport	Buses serve Puntagorda and Garafía from Los Llanos and Barlovento.

After leaving Puntagorda, crossing Barranco de Izcagua and skirting Las Tricias, the GR130 passes lots of dragon trees. Old mule tracks are linked across rugged barrancos, and a road-walk leads to the remote village of Garafía, or 'Santo Domingo' as it says on signposts.

The GR130 recommences where it crosses a steep road just above **Puntagorda**, passing between two houses. Follow an overgrown terrace below the main road and climb beside a water pipe. Cross a track and climb between two gardens, then turn left down an access road to a crossroads. Turn right uphill and follow a short path to the main road and a bus shelter. Cross over and a sign-post points up a path for La Rosa. Turn left along a track, Camino Real Rellanito, cross a road and go up Camino Real Barranquito Hondo. Walk straight ahead along a track, crossing a valley where there are a few dragon trees. Keep straight ahead along a terrace to the Centro de Naturaleza **La Rosa** and a campsite. ▶

Walk 28 crosses here.

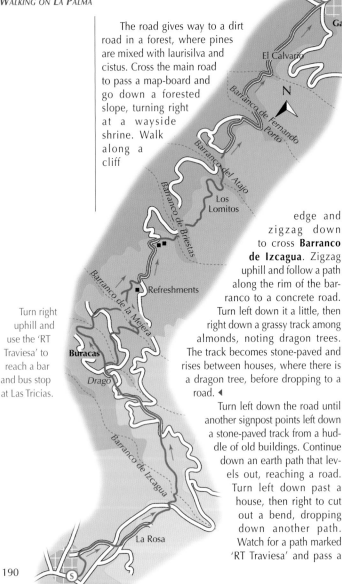

The road gives way to a dirt road in a forest, where pines are mixed with laurisilva and cistus. Cross the main road to pass a map-board and go down a forested slope, turning right at a wayside shrine. Walk along a cliff

edge and zigzag down to cross **Barranco de Izcagua**. Zigzag uphill and follow a path along the rim of the barranco to a concrete road. Turn left down it a little, then right down a grassy track among almonds, noting dragon trees. The track becomes stone-paved and rises between houses, where there is a dragon tree, before dropping to a road. ◄

Turn left down the road until another signpost points left down a stone-paved track from a huddle of old buildings. Continue down an earth path that levels out, reaching a road. Turn left down past a house, then right to cut out a bend, dropping down another path. Watch for a path marked 'RT Traviesa' and pass a

Turn right uphill and use the 'RT Traviesa' to reach a bar and bus stop at Las Tricias.

large and splendid dragon tree at **Drago**. Cross a road, use a short path, then cross a track and keep heading down as signposted 'RT Traviesa'. Watch for signs and markers, as there are two ways around **Buracas**, as follows.

A large dragon tree at Drago, the first of many passed around Buracas

Direct Route
Turn right along a terrace path, which dips into a valley to pass close to a pipe on an arch. Follow a track from a house to a road, crossing over to follow a path down among pines, reaching a three-way signpost in the rugged **Barranco de la Mejera**.

Variant Route
Drop down a steep, stone-paved path and pass several dragon trees to a small café. Turn right into a barranco full of caves, passing water troughs. Follow the path up rugged stone steps, past a dragon tree and over an odd cave dwelling. Turn right up a concrete road and left soon after. A narrow path traverses a grassy slope, down into and up from a barranco, then round and down to a three-way signpost in the rugged **Barranco de la Mejera**.

A narrow path crosses a steep slope near Lomada Grande

The two routes converge again here.

A house above may offer refreshments.

◄ Follow a fine stone-paved track up a slope of broom, turning right at the corner of a wall. Walk to the end of the wall and turn right uphill a short way, then left down a winding track. ◄ Turn right up a path to a road, then turn left down past the Km5 marker. Watch for a signpost after a few houses, on the right, revealing a path into the deep **Barranco de Briestas**. Note three large caves cut into crumbling ash on the far side. Go round a road bend, but before reaching the caves, turn right as signposted.

Zigzag up a stone-paved path, later hacked from red pumice, then cross a slope of almonds. Walk round a little valley, past a few pines, passing a gate at **Los Lomitos**. Turn left down a winding track, watching for a signpost on the right indicating a vague path to a telegraph pole. A clear stone-paved track zigzags into the deep and rugged **Barranco del Atajo**, popular with goats. Climb through a gate on the other side, passing a shrine at the top and continuing as signposted. Walk down a road to a junction and a bus shelter.

The last part is entirely along a road, so turn right and follow the road all the way round **Barranco de Fernando Porto**. The road rises and passes an old windmill at **El Calvario**, then descends and rises again to reach **Garafía**. There is a broad plaza and an old church, well worth looking inside. (Centro de Interpretación Ethnografico, bank with ATM, post office, shop, bars, buses and taxis).

WALK 40

GR130: Garafía to Franceses

Distance	17km (10½ miles)
Start	Garafía
Finish	Los Machines, Franceses
Total Ascent	1300m (4265ft)
Total Descent	1170m (3840ft)
Time	5hr
Terrain	Several rugged barrancos need to be crossed, using paths that are often rugged and very convoluted. Most slopes are scrub-covered but some are forested.
Refreshment	Bars at El Tablado.
Transport	Limited bus service between El Tablado and the main road. Buses serve Franceses from Garafía and Barlovento.

> The toughest part of the GR130 is along the northern coast. A succession of deep and steep-sided barrancos have to be crossed using convoluted paths. It all takes time, so give it plenty of time and enjoy the dramatic scenery, which changes constantly.

Walk straight through **Garafía** on a level road, through the plaza, to reach a map-board at the edge of the village. Turn right up to a signpost then left down a stone-paved path into **Barranco de la Luz** and up the other side. Dragon trees and cardón grow among the scrub. Follow a concrete track away from a house and continue along a short path, crossing a track and heading down through a gate. Join and follow a stone-paved path, curving round **Lomo Salvatierra** into a little valley.

Just above a small farm, walk straight ahead down a rugged path on a scrubby slope. Follow a fence and join a track, keeping straight ahead past cistus dotted with tree heather and straggly cornical. Go down a short-cut and stone steps, then follow the track onwards. There are dragon trees above and below, as well as lots of cardón

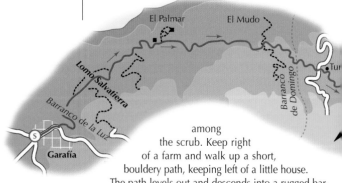

among the scrub. Keep right of a farm and walk up a short, bouldery path, keeping left of a little house. The path levels out and descends into a rugged barranco near El Palmar.

Climb from the barranco, pass a couple of houses and continue uphill. Pass under a pylon line and branch left along a path to reach a track. Climb and pass a junction with another track rising from El Mudo, then further up, a signpost points left up a rugged path. Cross a slope of heather and cistus then drop into the steep Barranco de Domingo. Go through a gate and zigzag up the other side, almost among laurisilva. Follow the path through a gate into a 'tunnel' formed by heather, and pass goat pens. Cross a track and a road to aim directly towards wind turbines.

Follow a track between the highest turbines, across a slope of heather trees, branching right at a poor marker up a clear path. Roughly contour and watch for hanging brambles. At the start of a zigzag descent there is a view from the coast all the way up to Roque de los Muchachos. Cross a brambly barranco and climb an ash path, which eases along the base of a cliff, then climbs to a couple of houses. Turn right to cross a concrete road, where Walk 24 joins, at **Don Pedro**. Turn sharp right at four odd dragon trees to follow a track that runs round and down the slopes of a valley. Walk down a bit of road past a couple of houses, then down steps to follow an easy terrace through heather, onto an open slope. Turn left down a track, pass a house with a dragon tree, then pass a few more houses. Walk 24 turns right uphill, while the GR130 turns left down to a picnic bench, cairn and mirador at **Miranda de La Calzada**.

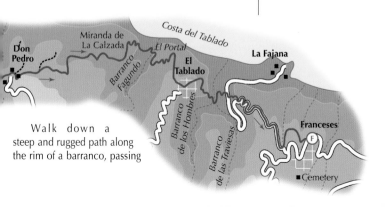

Walk down a steep and rugged path along the rim of a barranco, passing

The path zigzags in and out of the Barranco de los Hombres on the way to Franceses

Walk 26 joins at this point, while up the road there is a shop/bar, restaurant and occasional bus service.

dragon trees, cardón, tabaibal and prickly pears. Turn right to zigzag down into **Barranco Fagundo** and cross its bouldery bed. Climb a good path on the other side, passing cardón, and emerge at **El Portal**. Walk up a rugged path, passing between a few houses and dragon trees, then veer left round the foot of a stout, curved concrete wall to reach a signpost at **El Tablado**. ◄

Turn left a short way down a concrete road and right along a rugged path that narrows as it leaves the village. Drop down a narrow, stone-paved, vegetated path, zigzagging past a mirador into **Barranco de los Hombres**. Walk down the bouldery bed as if to follow a track, but turn right up a steep, winding path to cross a road.

Continue up a narrow, stone-paved, vegetated zigzag path. Reach a bendy road and turn left up it, reaching a valley and approaching houses. Watch for a concrete road down to the left and follow it, climbing a little past some houses. Continue down a track, but step right onto a path to walk round a valley where there are lots of dragon trees. Climb to a road at Los Machines, which is

part of **Franceses**. Unlikely as it may seem, a bus service squeezes along this road.

Looking up through the Barranco de las Traviesas on the climb to Franceses

WALK 41

GR130: Franceses to Los Sauces

Distance	18km (11 miles)
Start	Los Machines, Franceses
Finish	Los Sauces
Total Ascent	1000m (3280ft)
Total Descent	1220m (4000ft)
Time	6hr
Terrain	Easy roads and tracks alternate with steep and rugged paths across barrancos.
Refreshment	Bars at Gallegos, Barlovento and Los Sauces.
Transport	Buses serve Gallegos, Barlovento and Los Sauces from Garafía and Santa Cruz.

The GR130 continues through Gallegos, perched high between two deep barrancos. There are more barrancos to be crossed while turning the north-eastern corner of La Palma, but also easy walking near Barlovento. This stage ends in the bustling town of Los Sauces.

Start at Los Machines in **Franceses** and follow a narrow concrete road, which gives way to tarmac. The bus service follows this road, down and round a barranco, reaching a solitary house. Turn left down a concrete road and walk downhill, passing a B&B. Keep walking down a track, which begins to break up. Branch right and follow a winding track down through a gate. A mirador offers a fine view along the coast. Watch for a narrow, stony path heading left, then rugged zigzags drop into **Barranco de Franceses**, where there are masses of tabaibal and cardón.

Cross the barranco beside a cave and zigzag uphill, crossing the bare rock bed of a subsidiary barranco. Climb through a little gate and turn right. ◄ When a concrete track junction is reached, turn left to walk up between banana plantations and other plots. Pass a mapboard and walk up the steep Lomo de la Cancela into **Gallegos**.

Pass the Bar Viveres Gallegos and turn left opposite the 'Parada Taxi' sign, where the bus service turns. Go down a narrow and rugged path into a wonderfully scrubby barranco, passing caves near the bottom. Walk

Left is a restored path to Embarcadero de Gallegos, but if followed, steps must be retraced.

Map continues on page 201

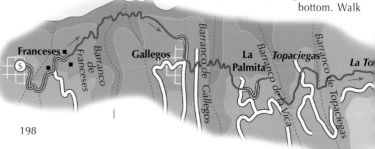

The descent into the deep and steep-sided Barranco de Gallegos

up the bed and turn left to zigzag up to a road. Cross over and walk down a track, initially fenced, rising through a gate, then drop into the deep and rugged **Barranco de Gallegos**. Cross the bouldery bed and zigzag up the other side, through patchy laurisilva. Climb, then turn left down a track past cultivated plots. Head up to a cross-track and walk ahead downhill. Watch for a path down to the left, swinging round a valley, climbing short and steep, levelling out towards a road junction above **La Palmita**.

Follow the middle of three roads, signposted GR130 for Barlovento, which becomes concrete down to a house. Walk down a path into **Barranco de la Vica**, roughly contouring across a slope of laurisilva, stout tabaibal and agaves. Cross the barranco and climb a

The Barranco de la Vica, between Gallegos and Barlovento

stone-paved path, which becomes rugged at a higher level. Exit to the left of a white electricity transformer tower. Walk down a concrete track and turn right along a path. Drop into **Barranco de Topaciegas**, where there is patchy laurisilva, and climb from it. Follow concrete roads as signposted to reach a lavadero.

Turn left along a concrete road, reach a building bearing a sign 'La Tosca', and turn right to walk along a terrace. Steps lead up to the Mirador de La Tosca beside the main road, but this is off-route. Turn right up a concrete road and left along the main road. Follow the old, bendy road, rather than the new road, to a crossroads and map-board on the outskirts of **Barlovento** (accommodation, banks with ATMs, post office, shops, bars, buses and taxis).

Walk straight through the crossroads to continue down the narrow Camino del Barranquito del Rey, later turning right as signposted for Los Sauces. Turn left up a road and continue straight along a grassy track, passing a signpost. Turn right along a road, which runs downhill a bit, then swings left to climb. Walk ahead and down to the end of the road. Don't turn right down a track, but go straight down a narrow, overgrown, brambly path to a road bend. Round the bend, a steep concrete road on the right climbs to a wide turning space on a gap beside **Montaña la Pitillera**. Don't turn left or right, but follow a track straight ahead, and watch for a path to the right. Pass patchy laurisilva and drop down a steep slope to a road. Turn right to follow the road round a left bend, reaching houses and a junction at **Lomo Romero**.

Turn left down a steep and narrow road, passing houses, gardens and little cultivated plots. Watch for a concrete path on the right, signposted Fuente de Gallega. A rugged path runs past this water source and a terrace leads to **Las Cabezadas**. Turn left down a steep road, passing houses, oranges and bananas, reaching a junction. Walk ahead along the Camino Real, where a house is built into an ash cone. Go down steps, following a steep and rugged zigzag path down a wonderfully scrubby slope. Things are difficult where a wet patch has rampant undergrowth. Turn right along the main road and left down a stone-paved track, onto a track in **Barranco de la Barata**.

Turn right and left to cross the barranco bed and climb past bananas to cross the main road again. Climb a zigzag path up a steep and scrubby slope. Climb a concrete ramp and keep straight ahead along a road overlooking the

Barranco de Topaciegas
La Tosca   **Barlovento**

N

▲ **Montaña la Pitillera**

Lomo Romero

Las Cabezadas

Barranco de la Barata

Los Sauces

F

barranco. Turn left along the road, where bananas fill the spaces between houses, and continue across a rise. Climb a flight of steps onto a little plaza at Cruz de la Lama. Turn right and climb gently up Calle Abraham Martin. Turn left along Calle Ciro Gonzalez, down to the plaza and church in **Los Sauces** (pensión, banks with ATMs, post office, shops, bars, buses and taxis).

WALK 42
GR130: Los Sauces to
Santa Cruz de La Palma

Distance	30km (18½ miles)
Start	Los Sauces
Finish	Santa Cruz
Total Ascent	1110m (3640ft)
Total Descent	1380m (4530ft)
Time	8hr
Terrain	Roads, tracks and paths, with a few steep and rugged barrancos.
Refreshment	Bars at San Andrés and Puntallana. Plenty of choice in Santa Cruz.
Transport	Buses serve San Andrés from Los Sauces. Buses serve Los Sauces, Puntallana, La Lomadita and Miranda from Barlovento and Santa Cruz.

The final stage of the GR130 is long, but not particularly hard. There are still some rugged barrancos, but also gentle roads, tracks and paths that can be covered at speed. If this stage needs to be broken, then Puntallana is halfway, and there are bus services at various points along the route.

Start on the far side of the plaza from the church in **Los Sauces**. Walk down the steep Camino la Calzada, swinging

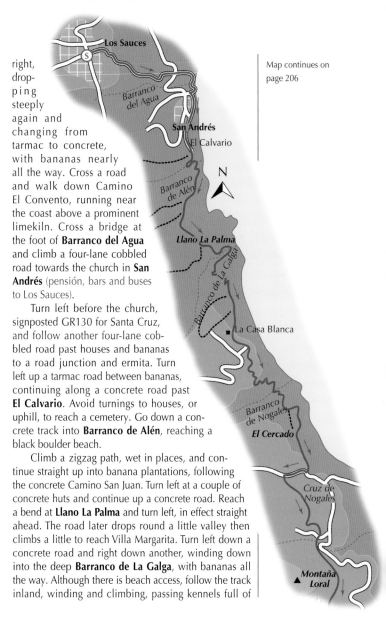

Map continues on
page 206

right,
drop-
ping
steeply
again and
changing from
tarmac to concrete,
with bananas nearly
all the way. Cross a road
and walk down Camino
El Convento, running near
the coast above a prominent
limekiln. Cross a bridge at
the foot of **Barranco del Agua**
and climb a four-lane cobbled
road towards the church in **San
Andrés** (pensión, bars and buses
to Los Sauces).

Turn left before the church,
signposted GR130 for Santa Cruz,
and follow another four-lane cobbled road past houses and bananas
to a road junction and ermita. Turn
left up a tarmac road between bananas,
continuing along a concrete road past
El Calvario. Avoid turnings to houses, or
uphill, to reach a cemetery. Go down a concrete track into **Barranco de Alén**, reaching a
black boulder beach.

Climb a zigzag path, wet in places, and continue straight up into banana plantations, following
the concrete Camino San Juan. Turn left at a couple of
concrete huts and continue up a concrete road. Reach
a bend at **Llano La Palma** and turn left, in effect straight
ahead. The road later drops round a little valley then
climbs a little to reach Villa Margarita. Turn left down a
concrete road and right down another, winding down
into the deep **Barranco de La Galga**, with bananas all
the way. Although there is beach access, follow the track
inland, winding and climbing, passing kennels full of

Looking back along the coast, from La Casa Blanca towards San Andrés

barking dogs in a cave. Emerge from the barranco and climb steeply along the rim.

Turn left along a narrow terrace path between veg-etables and bananas. Pass in front of a house, **La Casa Blanca**, to continue along and up a path with good coastal views. A signpost is reached at the foot of a very steep concrete road, but another path is indicated ahead. Turn quickly right and left onto a higher terrace, past bananas, then right and left to continue up concrete roads. Watch for a fenced path on the left, hugging the cliff-top, where mixed scrub contains fragrant incienso. Zigzag up to a concrete track and climb to a three-way signpost. ◄

Walk 33 joins here and La Galga is uphill.

Follow a fenced path past bananas, dipping in and out of a scrubby, stony little valley. Turn right up a concrete road to pass a banana tent, and turn left down a fenced path, zigzagging down to another three-way signpost. Keep ahead for the GR130, dropping more and more steeply along a convoluted, fenced path into **Barranco de Nogales**. The scrub includes broom, tabaibal, prickly pears, verode, calcosas, cornical, incienso, lavender, agaves and lots of cardón towards the bottom. Climb steps to follow a path with some fencing alongside. Zigzag to the top, reaching yet another three-way signpost.

Walk ahead and downhill beside a vineyard to and go down an overgrown path and steps, keeping seawards of bananas, later climbing. Curve inland from cliffs, beside vines, and turn left up a short, overgrown path to a higher track. Turn left to pass bananas, walking beside a plantation wall and turning right uphill beside it. Turn left down a path passing vines, not well marked, crossing a couple of little valleys. Walk up a concrete track to a house, then along a rugged stony track. Turn right along a short, walled track, then left down a road. Watch for a marker post and turn right up a path, between bananas and vines. Climb a steep concrete road, levelling out at a house near **Cruz de Nogales**. ▶

The road runs up to El Granel.

Just beyond the house, a path drops left, turning round a valley and rising across a scrubby slope. Fork left at a junction along an undulating, narrow and overgrown path. Continue gently up a track, left down a concrete road, and right along a narrow path across a scrubby slope. A short descent aided by a chain leads into the brambly Barranco de Los Tanques. Climb the other side and follow an overgrown path beside a stout wall. Turn right up a concrete road then left down a path to a picnic site on a road bend.

Don't step onto the road, but follow a fenced path across a scrubby ash slope on **Montaña Loral**, passing through a cultivated gap between two ash cones. Keep left at a track junction, overgrown, but better further uphill. Cross a couple of tracks and keep straight ahead. Turn right up a road to the Cupalma building, then right again up another road. Climb to a junction and turn left, steeper and steeper up Calle Procesiones, into **Puntallana**. There is a museum, Casa Luján, up to the right, but turn left to walk through the village (bank with ATM, post office, bars, shops and buses).

Walk along the road until a school is reached. A concrete road drops to the left opposite, between eucalyptus trees, signposted for Santa Cruz. Don't turn a left bend,

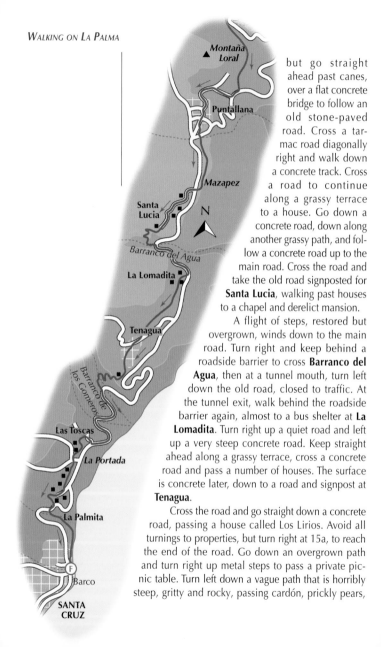

but go straight ahead past canes, over a flat concrete bridge to follow an old stone-paved road. Cross a tarmac road diagonally right and walk down a concrete track. Cross a road to continue along a grassy terrace to a house. Go down a concrete road, down along another grassy path, and follow a concrete road up to the main road. Cross the road and take the old road signposted for **Santa Lucia**, walking past houses to a chapel and derelict mansion.

A flight of steps, restored but overgrown, winds down to the main road. Turn right and keep behind a roadside barrier to cross **Barranco del Agua**, then at a tunnel mouth, turn left down the old road, closed to traffic. At the tunnel exit, walk behind the roadside barrier again, almost to a bus shelter at **La Lomadita**. Turn right up a quiet road and left up a very steep concrete road. Keep straight ahead along a grassy terrace, cross a concrete road and pass a number of houses. The surface is concrete later, down to a road and signpost at **Tenagua**.

Cross the road and go straight down a concrete road, passing a house called Los Lirios. Avoid all turnings to properties, but turn right at 15a, to reach the end of the road. Go down an overgrown path and turn right up metal steps to pass a private picnic table. Turn left down a vague path that is horribly steep, gritty and rocky, passing cardón, prickly pears,

The route passes close to the church in the village of Puntagorda

broom, tabaibal and tangled cornical. Watch for markers and don't short-cut. The path is fenced as it passes a cave. Go down to a track and walk to the main road.

Turn right to face the traffic, walking behind the roadside barrier round into **Barranco de los Gomeros**. Pass a monument and turn right up another road at **Las Toscas**. Turn sharp left up a concrete path and go down a concrete road. Walk round a tarmac bend to pass Bodegon El Sanavadit. Join and follow the main road downhill, and when it bends left, keep straight ahead up another road. Head right uphill, then left along the short, paved Calle Gotera. Walk off the end and down a concrete road, reaching a tunnel mouth and a roundabout.

Cross the road and pass a map-board, following the main road down towards Santa Cruz. Turn left down a path that zigzags into Barranco de El Dorador and walk down its bed. Follow a track on the right, and later keep right past a small industrial site. A road runs level past the Apartamentos Rocamar, joining the main road on the outskirts of **Santa Cruz**. Cross a river and head for the Barco, if that is where you started the GR130, or continue into town to finish at the Plaza de España.

WALK 43

GR131: Puerto de Tazacorte to
Roque de los Muchachos

Distance	17.5km (11 miles)
Start	Puerto de Tazacorte
Finish	Roque de los Muchachos
Total Ascent	2500m (8200ft)
Total Descent	75m (245ft)
Time	11hr
Terrain	Steep paths and tracks on cultivated slopes give way to steep paths on forested slopes, then rough and rocky paths on the highest mountains.
Refreshment	Bars at Puerto de Tazacorte. Bar at El Time.
Transport	Buses serve Puerto de Tazacorte and El Time from Los Llanos. No public transport to Roque de los Muchachos.

The GR131 through La Palma is the toughest long-distance trail in the Canary islands, and is generally covered in three to five days. The unrelenting climb from sea level at Puerto de Tazacorte to the highest point on La Palma, Roque de los Muchachos, is quite literally uphill all the way.

Start at the far end of **Puerto de Tazacorte** at the Kiosko Teneguia. Go up steps to a map-board and a stone-paved zigzag path. Climb past bananas, tabaibal and cardón, passing caves. The zigzags seem interminable but eventually reach the cliff-top. Climb a path to a junction beside an old Unipalma building. Walk up a narrow, overgrown, stone-paved track, and a concrete ramp leads onto a road. Turn right and left round a bend, and when the gradient eases, turn right up another steep, narrow road between banana tents. Swing right and left up dirt roads and another steep tarmac road, passing bananas and climbing a steep slope of tabaibal and prickly pears. Reach a main

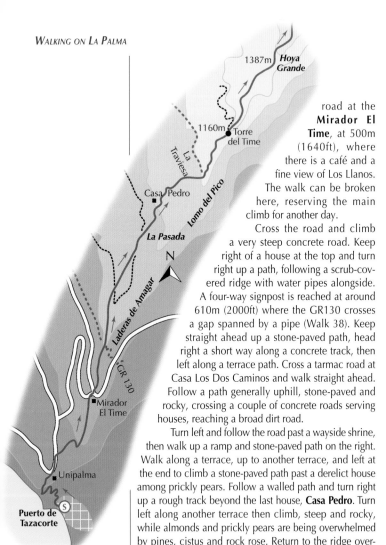

road at the **Mirador El Time**, at 500m (1640ft), where there is a café and a fine view of Los Llanos. The walk can be broken here, reserving the main climb for another day.

Cross the road and climb a very steep concrete road. Keep right of a house at the top and turn right up a path, following a scrub-covered ridge with water pipes alongside. A four-way signpost is reached at around 610m (2000ft) where the GR130 crosses a gap spanned by a pipe (Walk 38). Keep straight ahead up a stone-paved path, head right a short way along a concrete track, then left along a terrace path. Cross a tarmac road at Casa Los Dos Caminos and walk straight ahead. Follow a path generally uphill, stone-paved and rocky, crossing a couple of concrete roads serving houses, reaching a broad dirt road.

Turn left and follow the road past a wayside shrine, then walk up a ramp and stone-paved path on the right. Walk along a terrace, up to another terrace, and left at the end to climb a stone-paved path past a derelict house among prickly pears. Follow a walled path and turn right up a rough track beyond the last house, **Casa Pedro**. Turn left along another terrace then climb, steep and rocky, while almonds and prickly pears are being overwhelmed by pines, cistus and rock rose. Return to the ridge overlooking the deep Barranco de las Angustias, and roughly trace the ridge for the rest of the long ascent. Climb steeply to reach a signposted junction, around 1000m (3280ft), where the PR LP 10, La Traviesa, heads off left (Walk 22).

Map continues on page 212

Keep right for the GR131, up a broad and rocky path, steeply at first, crossing vine terraces later. Join a track, which is followed up to the right, with cistus and flowery scrub alongside. Reach a prominent fire tower and fenced mirador at **Torre del Time**, around 1160m (3805ft). Look down into the Caldera de Taburiente, sometimes filled with cloud, across to Pico Bejenado, and around the high mountains that will be traversed later.

A view from a gap across the Caldera de Taburiente to Pico Bejenado

The track drifts into a small valley, where the GR131 climbs a steep and rocky path, crossing a track and reaching it again later. Turn left to its end and continue along a path across terraces of vines and asphodel. Climb and contour among pines and rock rose to a gap at **Hoya Grande**, at 1387m (4550ft). The path twists and turns up the forested slope to a signpost. Keep climbing among pines, passing **Risco de Las Pareditas**, later reaching a gap. Make the most of views as there is a steep climb without any, before the gradient eases near a bare gap overlooking Tenerra. Zigzag up a steep and rocky slope, crossing a gap at **Hoya del Estrabito**, at 1920m (6300ft).

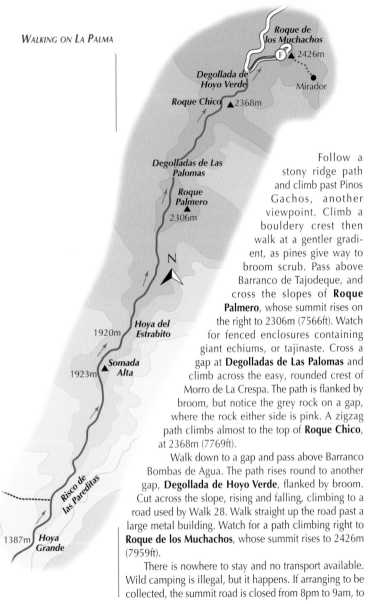

Follow a stony ridge path and climb past Pinos Gachos, another viewpoint. Climb a bouldery crest then walk at a gentler gradient, as pines give way to broom scrub. Pass above Barranco de Tajodeque, and cross the slopes of **Roque Palmero**, whose summit rises on the right to 2306m (7566ft). Watch for fenced enclosures containing giant echiums, or tajinaste. Cross a gap at **Degolladas de Las Palomas** and climb across the easy, rounded crest of Morro de La Crespa. The path is flanked by broom, but notice the grey rock on a gap, where the rock either side is pink. A zigzag path climbs almost to the top of **Roque Chico**, at 2368m (7769ft).

Walk down to a gap and pass above Barranco Bombas de Agua. The path rises round to another gap, **Degollada de Hoyo Verde**, flanked by broom. Cut across the slope, rising and falling, climbing to a road used by Walk 28. Walk straight up the road past a large metal building. Watch for a path climbing right to **Roque de los Muchachos**, whose summit rises to 2426m (7959ft).

There is nowhere to stay and no transport available. Wild camping is illegal, but it happens. If arranging to be collected, the summit road is closed from 8pm to 9am, to

Roque de los Muchachos, where the highest rocks are off-limits

avoid light pollution affecting nearby observatories. The highest rocks are crumbling and access is not permitted. Views stretch across La Palma and across the sea to the islands of El Hierro, La Gomera and Tenerife. There is a paved car park nearby, a national park information kiosk and water.

It is worth following a paved path down to a fine viewpoint (**mirador**) over the Caldera de Taburiente.

WALK 44

GR131: Roque de los Muchachos to Refugio del Pilar

Distance	26km (16 miles)
Start	Roque de los Muchachos
Finish	Refugio del Pilar recreation area
Total Ascent	600m (1970ft)
Total Descent	1550m (5085ft)
Time	11hr
Terrain	Rugged mountain paths, sometimes steep and rocky, but often gently graded. An easy forest road is used later.
Refreshment	Possible snack van at Refugio del Pilar.
Transport	No public transport.

Map continues on
page 216

Observatories

Los Andenes

N

Pared de
Roberto

2426m
*Roque de los
Muchachos*

2351m
*Pico
la C*

Mirador

The highest mountains on La Palma are very rocky, but walking from peak to peak is reasonably easy. The mountain crest is often sunny, even when it is misty and raining elsewhere on the island. This is a very long stage, slow in places, but faster once a dirt road is reached later.

*Steep red ash slopes
are crossed on way
down to Los Andenes*

Leave **Roque de los Muchachos**, at 2426m (7959ft), and follow a path down from a car park, signposted GR131 for Refugio del Pilar. Zigzag down to a gap at Degollada del Fraile, looking over the edge to see little shelters. Follow a stony, uneven path over a top, passing observatories. Cross a gap and pass Pico Fuente Nueva, at

2366m (7762ft), then go down a bouldery slope past a couple more **observatories**. The path drops through a gap in a wall-like dyke at **Pared de Roberto**, crossing crumbling slopes of ash to reach a road and mirador on a rocky gap at **Los Andenes**.

The path stays close to the road, undulates across a broad gap and climbs across a heap of boulders to a junction. ▶ Walk straight ahead along an easy, dusty, stony path, roughly following a fence, weaving between boulders and broom. The higher of the twin peaks of **Pico de la Cruz** bears a concrete hut at 2351m (7713ft). Enjoy views around La Palma, especially into the Caldera de Taburiente, and across the sea to El Hierro, La Gomera and Tenerife.

Zigzag down a gritty slope and continue more gently down the crest. The path rises and falls, avoiding summits, crossing scrubby slopes while pulling away from the road. Pass below **Pico de Piedra Llana** and the path zigzags down a scrubby slope. Cross a bare, rounded gap and rise to cut across the flanks of a couple of peaks, but watch for a path up to the right to the bare, stony top of **Pico de la Nieve**. Enjoy views from the summit cross and cairn at 2239m (7346ft). Retrace steps to continue down the GR131 to reach a signposted junction. ▶

The GR131 runs ahead down a stony path. Drop from the crest, zigzag down towards pines, and slice across the

Pico de Piedra Llana ▲ 2321m

Pico de la Nieve 2239m▲

Pico de la Sabina ▲ 2118m

Lomo Corralejo

Degollada del Río

Walks 29 and 30 head left for Barlovento and Los Sauces.

Walks 5 and 34 head left to Santa Cruz, Tenagua and Puntallana.

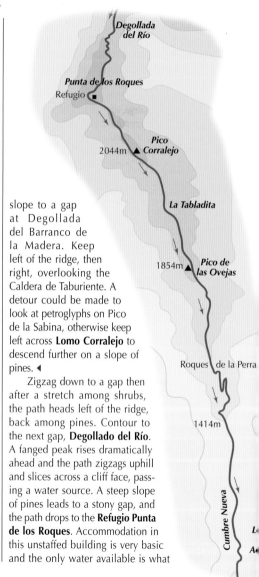

Broom and rock
rose flank the path,
and one peak ahead
deserves the name
'Half Dome', being
curved on one side
while dropping sheer
on the other.

slope to a gap
at Degollada
del Barranco de
la Madera. Keep
left of the ridge, then
right, overlooking the
Caldera de Taburiente. A
detour could be made to
look at petroglyphs on Pico
de la Sabina, otherwise keep
left across **Lomo Corralejo** to
descend further on a slope of
pines. ◄

Zigzag down to a gap then
after a stretch among shrubs,
the path heads left of the ridge,
back among pines. Contour to
the next gap, **Degollado del Río**.
A fanged peak rises dramatically
ahead and the path zigzags uphill
and slices across a cliff face, passing a water source. A steep slope
of pines leads to a stony gap, and
the path drops to the **Refugio Punta
de los Roques**. Accommodation in
this unstaffed building is very basic
and the only water available is what

drains from the roof. Enjoy views ahead to the Cumbre Nueva and Cumbre Vieja.

Zigzag down a steep slope of pines to a gap. Climb a rough and stony path, aiming towards a rocky tower, but when a gap is reached, head right beside a rock wall. Reach another gap at a sign for **Pico Corralejo**, where there is an option to climb to its summit trig point at 2044m (6,706ft). The GR131 continues along the crest then zigzags down among pines. The route stays on or near the crest, flanked by rock rose, undulating close to **Pico de las Ovejas**, whose 1854m (6082ft) summit is just to the right, passed by Walk 3. Later, zigzag down a steeper, rockier part of the crest, still among pines and rock rose, but with clumps of heather alongside. More zigzags drop past **Roques de La Perra**, landing on a clear track.

The track falls and rises, swings sharply left and right downhill, becoming bendy among pines and laurisilva, reaching a sharp bend before a junction on the **Cumbre Nueva** at 1414m 4639ft). The coast-to-coast PR LP 1 (Walk 6) crosses here, and a monument commemorates the island-hopping GR131 and its incorporation into the pan-European E7 route. There is a choice, either to follow the track straight ahead, or use paths signposted to right and left of it.

The track undulates gently, ▶ often flanked by dense laurisilva, and cloud may cover it. Communication masts stand on top of **Reventón** at 1435m (4708ft) and the track rises and falls gently across its slopes.

A small open refuge offers shelter alongside.

The route passes Pico del Cedro on its way to the Refugio Punta de los Roques

Alternatively, paths run parallel to the track most of the way. Watch for markers and signposts to spot them. The track gently undulates and generally climbs to reach a mapboard on a road bend. Turn right to walk down through a cutting to find **Refugio del Pilar** among pines on the left, around 1455m (4775ft). This is a recreation area with a small visitor centre and campsite, ideally suited for breaking this long trail, and a hub for Walks 7, 8, 9, 10 and 11.

WALK 45

GR131: Refugio del Pilar to Faro de Fuencaliente

Distance	24.5km (15¼ miles)
Start	Refugio del Pilar
Finish	Faro de Fuencaliente
Total Ascent	600m (1970ft)
Total Descent	2150m (7055ft)
Time	8hr
Terrain	Several ascents and descents on slopes of volcanic ash and lava, sometimes forested, sometimes barren, finishing on the coast.
Refreshment	Possible snack van at Refugio del Pilar. Bars at Fuencaliente. Restaurant near Faro de Fuencaliente.
Transport	Taxi to start. Buses serve Fuencaliente from Santa Cruz and Los Llanos. Buses serve Faro de Fuencaliente from Fuencaliente.

The last day's walk in this book covers the most recent landscapes on La Palma. Volcanic eruptions in recent centuries have added extra peaks to the Cumbre Vieja. The GR131 follows the Ruta de los Volcánes to Fuencaliente and down to the most southerly point on the island.

Leave **Refugio del Pilar**, at 1455m (4775ft), from behind the visitor centre, where there is a map-board. The GR131 climbs a broad and clear path on the right, winding among dense pines to **Mirador del Birigoyo**. There is a view out of the trees to Montaña Quemada, which erupted in 1480. Continue up the path, past a three-way signpost, which offers an ascent of Pico Birigoyo, otherwise stay on the main path, passing tagasaste bushes among pines. Turn a corner and follow the path downhill as the pines thin out, reaching another three-way signpost on a slope of ash and rocks.

Turn left up a broad track across a steep slope of broken lava, heading back among pines. Climb across

Walking down through a valley of soft volcanic ash after passing Collado de las Deseadas

the flank **of Montaña la Barquita**, passing another three-way signpost, keeping right to stay on the GR131. Pass curious stone spirals in the forest, where broom and rock rose grow. Follow the path up across the flank of **Montaña de los Charcos**, passing another curious stone spiral. Rise and fall across slopes of pines and bare ash, crossing a footbridge over a gully, then wind up a stony ash path. Yet another three-way signpost is reached, at around 1875m (6150ft), near **Pico Nambroque**. ◄

Eruptions occurred nearby, in 1585 at Volcán Tajuya, and 1949 at Hoyo Negro.

Continue straight up the stony crest, over a rise and down a little, then either detour right for **Hoyo Negro**, or continue up and along the path, through a stand of pines. There is later a view down to the dark, thick, **Lavas del Duraznero**, which the path crosses on a gap, passing fissures and blocks. The GR131 heads down to the right and later climbs towards **Volcán Deseada**, but it is worth leaving the trail and making a direct ascent, as the volcanic scenery is remarkable. Either way, be sure to climb to the trig point at 1931m (6335ft) to inspect the crater. The far side of the rim rises to

1949m (6394ft). Views stretch across La Palma to the islands of El Hierro, La Gomera, with El Teide rising above Tenerife.

Follow a loose, gritty, stony path down the ridge, passing pines at the bottom. Continue along the crest, reaching a junction on an ash gap, **Collado de las Deseadas**, at 1828m (5997ft). Walk 12 crosses here, while the GR131 runs gently uphill. Later, descend through a long, shallow, grey ash valley, where the path is very loose. Tall pines are passed towards the end and the path rises gently from a signpost on a stonier slope. A gentle gap is crossed at **Llano de la Manteca**, and looking ahead, the colourful cone of **Volcán Martín** is seen and the path runs towards its slopes The volcano erupted in 1646, and although off-route, is worth exploring. The crater contains a cave with a hidden water source.

The GR131 slices across stony slopes, crosses a gentle gap and runs down an ash slope. Fuente del Tión lies off-route nearby, otherwise stay on the main path down a loose ash slope, avoiding turnings and watching for signposts. The path drifts right towards a blocky lava flow, then left gently downhill. Cross a track, **Vereda de las Cabras**, and undulate across forested mounds of ash. Walk beside the lava flow and drop down beside **Montaña del Fuego** to pass another signpost, keeping straight ahead. Contour across a steep slope, then at another signpost, descend gently on slopes of ash and pines. The path is broad and flanked by parallel lines of stones. Look ahead to spot a prominent mast and cross a track before it.

Follow the path as it swings right of **Montaña del Pino** and its mast, crossing its access track. A rough and rocky path drops through forest, crossing

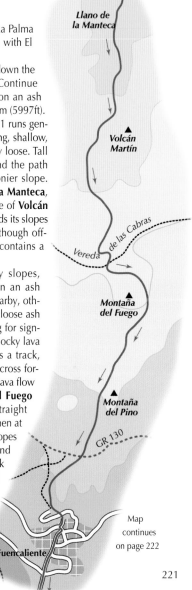

Llano de la Manteca

Volcán Martín

Vereda de las Cabras

Montaña del Fuego

Montaña del Pino

GR130

Fuencaliente

Map continues on page 222

221

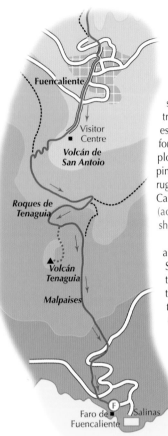

another track, and is enclosed by stone walls for a while. Pass a small area planted with vines and go straight down through an intersection with the GR130 (Walk 36). Cross a track and follow a walled path down the forested slope. Turn left as signposted down to a forest road, which descends gently past cultivated plots. Turn left down a rugged, gritty path, dropping to a broad dirt road. Go down a short, steep rugged path to a church, and walk straight down Calle Jose Pons to the main road in **Fuencaliente** (accommodation, bank with ATM, post office, shops, bars, buses and taxis).

Find the Bar Parada on the main road and go straight down Calle Emilio Quintana Sanchez. Continue down round a bend, then turn right down Calle los Volcánes. Go straight through a crossroads and pass a map-board to reach **Volcán de San Antonio**. The volcano erupted in 1677 and a visitor centre with a café lies beneath the crater rim. There is an entry charge for the visitor centre, but not to follow the GR131, which turns down to the right beforehand.

A loose ash path is signposted down a slope of pines and vines. Turn left along a firm ash road and walk gently down across steep ash slopes dotted with calcosas bushes. Paths allow a diversion off-route to the colourful Roques de Teneguía. The ash road reaches a junction where a right turn leads down to a parking space. Turn left, and although the GR131 is marked down to the left at a junction, it is worth keeping right to visit the chaotic **Volcan Teneguía**, which erupted in 1971. Both the crater and 427m (1401ft) summit can be inspected. There were 'hot spots' in the crater a few years ago, but these have cooled.

Back on the GR131, the path passes a small crater and runs down beside a blocky lava flow, with vines

The Faro de Fuencaliente and nearby salinas at the end of the trail

nearby. Cut across the lava flow then drop steeply down barren grey ash and pumice, dotted with scrub and occasionally tinged red. Walk through a defile full of shrubby salado to reach a road, turning right to follow it a short way. Watch for a signpost and markers as the path drops left, passing cabbage-like *lechugas*. Cross the road and follow the path downhill. Cross the road again for the final descent to **Faro de Fuencaliente**.

A red and white lighthouse stands beside an older restored structure. Beyond the lighthouses are interesting and intricate *salinas*, or salt pans overlooked by a restaurant. Beyond them are the southernmost cliffs on La Palma, so retrace steps to the lighthouses and wait for a bus back to Fuencaliente. The GR131 raverses all seven of the Canary Islands, so there is plenty more to explore.

APPENDIX A

Route summary table

Walk no	Start	Finish	Distance	Time	Total Ascent	Total Descent	Page
1	Santa Cruz/ Santuario de las Nieve	Santa Cruz/ Santuario de las Nieve	8/11/19km (5/7/12 miles)	2hr30/4hr/ 6hr30	410/1180/1590m (1345/3870/5215ft)	410/1180/1590m (1345/3870/5215ft)	30
2	Breña Alta	Breña Alta	10km (6¼ miles)	2hr45	550m (1805ft)	550m (1805ft)	35
3	Restaurante La Graja, Buenavista	Restaurante Los Almendros, Velhoco	13km (8 miles)	5hr	1550m (5085ft)	1590m (5215ft)	38
4	Barco, Santa Cruz	Barco, Santa Cruz	15km (9½ miles)	5hr	1150m (3770ft)	1150m (3770ft)	42
5	Mountain road between Km24 and Km25	Barco, Santa Cruz	6/14/20km (3¾/8¾/ 12½ miles)	2hr30/4hr30/ 7hr	60/340/400m (195/1115/1310ft)	340/1960/2300m (1115/6430/7545ft)	45
6	Plaza de España, Santa Cruz	Puerto de Tazacorte	31km (19¼ miles)	9hr	1500m (4920ft)	1500m (4920ft)	49
7	Centro de Visitantes, El Paso	Refugio del Pilar	7km (4½ miles)	2hr	635m (2085ft)	-	54
8	Refugio del Pilar	Harbour, Santa Cruz	10.5–16km (6½–10 miles)	3hr30–5hr	-	1250/1550m (4100/5085ft)	56

Walk no	Start	Finish	Distance	Time	Total Ascent	Total Descent	Page
9	Refugio del Pilar	Playa del Hoyo or the airport	15km (9½ miles)	4hr30	-	1455m (4775ft)	63
10	Refugio del Pilar	Playa del Hoyo or La Salamera	15km (9½ miles)	5hr	150m (490ft)	1700m (5575ft)	67
11	Refugio del Pilar	Refugio del Pilar	12km (7½ miles)	4hr	350m (1150ft)	350m (1150ft)	72
12	Jedey	Tigalate	22km (13½ miles)	6hr	1230m (4035ft)	1130m (3710ft)	75
13	San Nicolás	San Nicolás	10km (6 miles)	3hr	600m (1970ft)	600m (1970ft)	79
14	Llanos del Jable	Llanos del Jable	11km (7 miles)	3hr30	600m (1970ft)	600m (1970ft)	82
15	La Cumbrecita or El Barrial	La Cumbrecita or El Barrial	8/10.5km (5/6½ miles)	3/4hr	600/800m (1970/2625ft)	600/800m (1970/2625ft)	87
16	La Cumbrecita	Los Llanos	12km (7½ miles)	7hr	600m (1970ft)	1555m (5100ft)	90
17	Los Llanos/Los Brecitos	Los Llanos/ Barranco de las Angustias	14/27km (8¾/16¾ miles)	4hr30/9hr30	200/1400m (655/4595ft)	1080/1400m (3545/4595ft)	93

Walk no	Start	Finish	Distance	Time	Total Ascent	Total Descent	Page
18	La Cumbrecita	Campsite, Caldera de Taburiente	13km (8 miles)	7hr	500m (1640ft)	1060m (3480ft)	99
19	Campsite, Caldera de Taburiente	Campsite, Caldera de Taburiente	6.5km (4 miles)	4hr	700m (2295ft)	700m (2295ft)	103
20	Tijarafe	Tijarafe	10km (6¼ miles)	3hr30	850m (2790ft)	850m (2790ft)	105
21	Tinizara	Tijarafe	15km (9½ miles)	5hr	1000m (3215ft)	1250m (4100ft)	108
22	Mirador de El Time	Kiosko Briesta	30km (18¾ miles)	8hr	1330m (4365ft)	630m (2065ft)	112
23	Kiosko Briesta	Barlovento	32km (20 miles)	8hr	660m (2165ft)	1270m (4165ft)	117
24	Parque Cultural La Zarza	Parque Cultural La Zarza	9/15km (5½/9½ miles)	2hr30/4hr	400/850m (1310/2790ft)	400/850m (1310/2790ft)	123
25	Roque del Faro	Garafía	15km (9½ miles)	4hr	100m (330ft)	750m (2460ft)	127
26	Roque del Faro	Roque del Faro	19km (12 miles)	6hr	1150m (3770ft)	1150m (3770ft)	130
27	Roque del Faro	Roque de los Muchachos	12km (7½ miles)	4hr	1525m (5005ft)	100m (330ft)	134

Walk no	Start	Finish	Distance	Time	Total Ascent	Total Descent	Page
28	Roque de los Muchachos	Puntagorda/Tijarafe	17km (10½ miles)	5hr	50m (165ft)	1675/1825m (5495/5990ft)	138
29	Roadside below Pico de la Cruz	Barlovento	17km (10½ miles)	5hr	75m (245ft)	1775m (5825ft)	142
30	Roadside below Pico de la Cruz	Los Sauces	17/19km (10½/12 miles)	5/6hr	75/225m (245/740ft)	1985/2165m (6510/7105ft)	146
31	Los Sauces/Casa del Monte	Los Tilos/Los Sauces	10/16/26km (6¼/10/16 miles)	4hr/5hr30/9hr	350/500/1600m (1150/1640/5250ft)	350/500/1600m (1150/1640/5250ft)	151
32	Fuente de Olén	Las Lomadas	19km (12 miles)	5hr	300m (985ft)	1770m (5810ft)	156
33	Fuente Vizcaína	La Galga	13/15/19km (8/9½/12 miles)	4hr/4hr30/6hr	50/300m (165/985ft)	1750/2050m (5740/6725ft)	160
34	Mountain road between Km24 and Km25	Puntallana	16/22km (10/13¾ miles)	4hr30/7hr	35/375m (115/1230ft)	1535/1910m (5035/6265ft)	165
35	Santa Cruz	Villa de Mazo	14km (8¾ miles)	4hr	700m (2295ft)	100m (330ft)	170
36	Villa de Mazo	Fuencaliente	19km (12 miles)	5hr	500m (1640ft)	300m (985ft)	173
37	Fuencaliente	Los Llanos de Aridane	27km (17 miles)	7hr	350m (1150ft)	700m (2300ft)	177

Walk no	Start	Finish	Distance	Time	Total Ascent	Total Descent	Page
38	Los Llanos de Aridane	Puntagorda	25km (15½ miles)	7hr30	1400m (4595ft)	1000m (3280ft)	183
39	Puntagorda	Garafía	17km (10½ miles)	4hr	400m (1310ft)	780m (2560ft)	189
40	Garafía	Los Machines, Franceses	17km (10½ miles)	5hr	1300m (4265ft)	1170m (3840ft)	193
41	Los Machines, Franceses	Los Sauces	18km (11 miles)	6hr	1000m (3280ft)	1220m (4000ft)	197
42	Los Sauces	Santa Cruz	30km (18½ miles)	8hr	1110m (3640ft)	1380m (4530ft)	202
43	Puerto de Tazacorte	Roque de los Muchachos	17.5km (11 miles)	11hr	2500m (8200ft)	75m (245ft)	209
44	Roque de los Muchachos	Refugio del Pilar	26km (16 miles)	11hr	600m (1970ft)	1550m (5085ft)	213
45	Refugio del Pilar	Faro de Fuencaliente	24.5km (15¼ miles)	8hr	600m (1970ft)	2150m (7055ft)	218

APPENDIX B

Topographical glossary

Apart from a few place-names derived from original Guanche words, most names appearing on maps are Spanish. Many words appear frequently and are usually descriptive of landforms or colours. The following list of common words helps to sort out what some of the places on maps or signposts mean.

Spanish	English	Spanish	English
agua	water	*gordo*	fat/giant
alto/alta	high	*grande*	big
arenas	sands	*guagua*	bus
arroyo	stream	*hoya*	valley
asomada	promontory	*ladera*	slope
bajo/baja	low	*llano*	plain
barranco	ravine	*lomo*	spur/ridge
barranquillo	small ravine	*montaña*	mountain
blanco/blanca	white	*morro*	nose
boca	gap	*negro/negra*	black
cabeza	head	*nieve*	snow
caldera	crater	*nuevo/nueva*	new
calle	street	*parada*	bus stop
camino	path/track	*paso*	pass
cañada	gully	*pequeño*	small
canal	watercourse	*pico*	peak
carretera	road	*piedra*	rock
casa	house	*pino/pinar*	pine
casa forestal	forestry house	*playa*	beach
caseta	small house/hut	*plaza*	town square
collada/degollada	col/gap/saddle	*presa*	small reservoir
colorada	coloured	*puerto*	port
cruz	cross/crossroads	*punta*	point
cueva	cave	*risco*	cliff
cumbre	ridge/crest	*roja*	red
de/del	of the	*roque*	rock
el/la/los/las	the	*san/santa*	saint (male/female)
embalse	reservoir	*sendero*	route/path
era	threshing floor	*valle*	valley
ermita	chapel/shrine	*verde*	green
estacion de guaguas	bus station	*vieja/viejo*	old
fuente	fountain/spring	*volcán*	volcano

APPENDIX C
Useful contacts

Inter-island Flights
Binter Canarias, tel 902 391 392,
www.bintercanarias.com
Canaryfly, tel 902 808 065, www.canaryfly.es

Inter-island Ferries
Lineas Fred Olsen, tel 902 100 107,
www.fredolsen.es
Naviera Armas, tel 902 456 500,
www.navieraarmas.com

Bus Services
Tenerife TITSA, tel 922 531 300,
www.titsa.com
Transportes Insular de La Palma, tel 922 411 924
or 922 414 411, www.transporteslapalma.com

Canary Islands Tourism
General Canary Islands tourism
www.holaislascanarias.com

La Palma tourism
www.visitlapalma.es

Tourist Information Offices
Santa Cruz, tel 922 412 106
Los Llanos, tel 922 490 072
Mazo, tel 922 967 044
El Paso, tel 922 485 733
Breña Baja, tel 922 181 354
Tazacorte, tel 922 480 803
Fuencaliente, tel 615 390 616

Island Government (Cabildo)
Cabildo de La Palma www.cabildodelapalma.es

After leaving the Refugio Punta de los Roques the route heads towards a rock tower (Walk 44)

Free Trails Map
La Palma   www.senderosdelapalma.es

National Park
Caldera de Taburiente, www.gobiernodecanarias.org/
parquesnacionalesdecanarias/en/CalderaTaburiente

NOTES

NOTES

NOTES

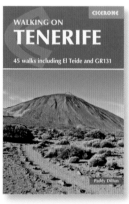

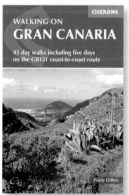

LISTING OF CICERONE GUIDES

SCOTLAND

Backpacker's Britain:
  Northern Scotland
Ben Nevis and Glen Coe
Cycling in the Hebrides
Great Mountain Days in Scotland
Mountain Biking in Southern and
  Central Scotland
Mountain Biking in West and North
  West Scotland
Not the West Highland Way
Scotland
Scotland's Best Small Mountains
Scotland's Mountain Ridges
Scrambles in Lochaber
The Ayrshire and Arran
  Coastal Paths
The Border Country
The Cape Wrath Trail
The Great Glen Way
The Great Glen Way Map Booklet
The Hebridean Way
The Hebrides
The Isle of Mull
The Isle of Skye
The Skye Trail
The Southern Upland Way
The Speyside Way
The Speyside Way Map Booklet
The West Highland Way
Walking Highland Perthshire
Walking in Scotland's Far North
Walking in the Angus Glens
Walking in the Cairngorms
Walking in the Ochils, Campsie
  Fells and Lomond Hills
Walking in the Pentland Hills
Walking in the Southern Uplands
Walking in Torridon
Walking Loch Lomond and
  the Trossachs
Walking on Arran
Walking on Harris and Lewis
Walking on Rum and the
  Small Isles
Walking on the Orkney and
  Shetland Isles
Walking on Uist and Barra
Walking the Corbetts
  Vol 1 South of the Great Glen
Walking the Corbetts
  Vol 2 North of the Great Glen
Walking the Galloway Hills
Walking the Munros
  Vol 1 – Southern, Central and
  Western Highlands

Walking the Munros
  Vol 2 – Northern Highlands and
  the Cairngorms
West Highland Way Map Booklet
Winter Climbs Ben Nevis and
  Glen Coe
Winter Climbs in the Cairngorms

NORTHERN ENGLAND TRAILS

Hadrian's Wall Path
Hadrian's Wall Path Map Booklet
Pennine Way Map Booklet
The Coast to Coast Map Booklet
The Coast to Coast Walk
The Dales Way
The Dales Way Map Booklet
The Pennine Way

LAKE DISTRICT

Cycling in the Lake District
Great Mountain Days in the
  Lake District
Lake District Winter Climbs
Lake District: High Level and
  Fell Walks
Lake District: Low Level and
  Lake Walks
Mountain Biking in the Lake District
Scrambles in the Lake District
  – North
Scrambles in the Lake District
  – South
Short Walks in Lakeland Books 1–3
The Cumbria Way
Tour of the Lake District
Trail and Fell Running in the
  Lake District

NORTH WEST ENGLAND
AND THE ISLE OF MAN

Cycling the Pennine Bridleway
Cycling the Way of the Roses
Isle of Man Coastal Path
The Lancashire Cycleway
The Lune Valley and Howgills
The Ribble Way
Walking in Cumbria's Eden Valley
Walking in Lancashire
Walking in the Forest of Bowland
  and Pendle
Walking on the Isle of Man
Walking on the West
  Pennine Moors
Walks in Lancashire Witch Country
Walks in Ribble Country
Walks in Silverdale and Arnside

NORTH EAST ENGLAND,
YORKSHIRE DALES AND
PENNINES

Cycling in the Yorkshire Dales
Great Mountain Days in
  the Pennines
Mountain Biking in the
  Yorkshire Dales
South Pennine Walks
St Oswald's Way and
  St Cuthbert's Way
The Cleveland Way and the
  Yorkshire Wolds Way
The Cleveland Way Map Booklet
The North York Moors
The Reivers Way
The Teesdale Way
Walking in County Durham
Walking in Northumberland
Walking in the North Pennines
Walking in the Yorkshire Dales:
  North and East
Walking in the Yorkshire Dales:
  South and West
Walks in Dales Country
Walks in the Yorkshire Dales

WALES AND WELSH BORDERS

Cycling Lôn Las Cymru
Glyndwr's Way
Great Mountain Days in Snowdonia
Hillwalking in Shropshire
Hillwalking in Wales – Vols 1 & 2
Mountain Walking in Snowdonia
Offa's Dyke Map Booklet
Offa's Dyke Path
Pembrokeshire Coast Path
  Map Booklet
Ridges of Snowdonia
Scrambles in Snowdonia
The Ascent of Snowdon
The Ceredigion and Snowdonia
  Coast Paths
The Pembrokeshire Coast Path
The Severn Way
The Snowdonia Way
The Wales Coast Path
The Wye Valley Walk
Walking in Carmarthenshire
Walking in Pembrokeshire
Walking in the Forest of Dean
Walking in the South Wales Valleys
Walking in the Wye Valley
Walking on the Brecon Beacons
Walking on the Gower
Welsh Winter Climbs

DERBYSHIRE, PEAK DISTRICT AND MIDLANDS

Cycling in the Peak District
Dark Peak Walks
Scrambles in the Dark Peak
Walking in Derbyshire
White Peak Walks:
  The Northern Dales
White Peak Walks:
  The Southern Dales

SOUTHERN ENGLAND

20 Classic Sportive Rides
  in South East England
20 Classic Sportive Rides
  in South West England
Cycling in the Cotswolds
Mountain Biking on the
  North Downs
Mountain Biking on the
  South Downs
North Downs Way Map Booklet
South West Coast Path Map Booklet
  – Vols 1–3
Suffolk Coast and Heath Walks
The Cotswold Way
The Cotswold Way Map Booklet
The Great Stones Way
The Kennet and Avon Canal
The Lea Valley Walk
The North Downs Way
The Peddars Way and Norfolk
  Coast Path
The Pilgrims' Way
The Ridgeway Map Booklet
The Ridgeway National Trail
The South Downs Way
The South Downs Way
  Map Booklet
The South West Coast Path
The Thames Path
The Thames Path Map Booklet
The Two Moors Way
Walking Hampshire's Test Way
Walking in Cornwall
Walking in Essex
Walking in Kent
Walking in London
Walking in Norfolk
Walking in Sussex
Walking in the Chilterns
Walking in the Cotswolds
Walking in the Isles of Scilly
Walking in the New Forest
Walking in the North
  Wessex Downs
Walking in the Thames Valley
Walking on Dartmoor
Walking on Guernsey
Walking on Jersey
Walking on the Isle of Wight

Walking the Jurassic Coast
Walks in the South Downs
  National Park

BRITISH ISLES CHALLENGES, COLLECTIONS AND ACTIVITIES

The Book of the Bivvy
The Book of the Bothy
The C2C Cycle Route
The End to End Cycle Route
The Mountains of England and
  Wales: Vol 1 Wales
The Mountains of England and
  Wales: Vol 2 England
The National Trails
The UK's County Tops
Three Peaks, Ten Tors

ALPS CROSS-BORDER ROUTES

100 Hut Walks in the Alps
Across the Eastern Alps: E5
Alpine Ski Mountaineering Vol 1 –
  Western Alps
Alpine Ski Mountaineering Vol 2 –
  Central and Eastern Alps
Chamonix to Zermatt
The Karnischer Hohenweg
The Tour of the Bernina
Tour of Mont Blanc
Tour of Monte Rosa
Tour of the Matterhorn
Trail Running – Chamonix and the
  Mont Blanc region
Trekking in the Alps
Trekking in the Silvretta and
  Rätikon Alps
Trekking Munich to Venice
Walking in the Alps

PYRENEES AND FRANCE/SPAIN CROSS-BORDER ROUTES

The GR10 Trail
The GR11 Trail
The Pyrenean Haute Route
The Pyrenees
The Way of St James – Spain
Walks and Climbs in the Pyrenees

AUSTRIA

Innsbruck Mountain Adventures
The Adlerweg
Trekking in Austria's Hohe Tauern
Trekking in the Stubai Alps
Trekking in the Zillertal Alps
Walking in Austria

SWITZERLAND

Cycle Touring in Switzerland
The Swiss Alpine Pass Route –
  Via Alpina Route 1
The Swiss Alps

Tour of the Jungfrau Region
Walking in the Bernese Oberland
Walking in the Valais
Walks in the Engadine –
  Switzerland

FRANCE

Chamonix Mountain Adventures
Cycle Touring in France
Cycling London to Paris
Cycling the Canal du Midi
Écrins National Park
Mont Blanc Walks
Mountain Adventures in the
  Maurienne
The GR20 Corsica
The GR5 Trail
The GR5 Trail – Vosges and Jura
The Grand Traverse of the
  Massif Central
The Loire Cycle Route
The Moselle Cycle Route
The River Rhone Cycle Route
The Robert Louis Stevenson Trail
The Way of St James – Le Puy to
  the Pyrenees
Tour of the Oisans: The GR54
Tour of the Queyras
Vanoise Ski Touring
Via Ferratas of the French Alps
Walking in Corsica
Walking in Provence – East
Walking in Provence – West
Walking in the Auvergne
Walking in the Briançonnais
Walking in the Cevennes
Walking in the Dordogne
Walking in the Haute Savoie: North
Walking in the Haute Savoie: South
Walks in the Cathar Region

GERMANY

Hiking and Biking in the
  Black Forest
The Danube Cycleway Volume 1
The Rhine Cycle Route
The Westweg
Walking in the Bavarian Alps

ICELAND AND GREENLAND

Walking and Trekking in Iceland

IRELAND

The Irish Coast to Coast Walk
The Mountains of Ireland
The Wild Atlantic Way and
  Western Ireland

ITALY

Italy's Sibillini National Park
Shorter Walks in the Dolomites

Ski Touring and Snowshoeing in
    the Dolomites
The Way of St Francis
Through the Italian Alps
Trekking in the Apennines
Trekking in the Dolomites
Via Ferratas of the Italian
    Dolomites: Vol 1
Via Ferratas of the Italian
    Dolomites: Vol 2
Walking and Trekking in the
    Gran Paradiso
Walking in Abruzzo
Walking in Italy's Stelvio
    National Park
Walking in Sardinia
Walking in Sicily
Walking in the Dolomites
Walking in Tuscany
Walking in Umbria
Walking on the Amalfi Coast
Walking the Italian Lakes
Walks and Treks in the
    Maritime Alps

BELGIUM AND LUXEMBOURG

The GR5 Trail – Benelux and
    Lorraine
Walking in the Ardennes

SCANDINAVIA

Walking in Norway

**EASTERN EUROPE AND THE
BALKANS**

The Danube Cycleway Volume 2
The High Tatras
The Mountains of Romania
Walking in Bulgaria's
    National Parks
Walking in Hungary
Mountain Biking in Slovenia
The Islands of Croatia
The Julian Alps of Slovenia
The Mountains of Montenegro
The Peaks of the Balkans Trail
Trekking in Slovenia
Walking in Croatia
Walking in Slovenia:
    The Karavanke

SPAIN AND PORTUGAL

Coastal Walks in Andalucia
Cycle Touring in Spain
Mountain Walking in Mallorca
Mountain Walking in
    Southern Catalunya
Spain's Sendero Histórico: The GR1
The Andalucian Coast to
    Coast Walk
The Mountains of Nerja

The Mountains of Ronda
    and Grazalema
The Northern Caminos
The Sierras of Extremadura
Trekking in Mallorca
Walking and Trekking in the
    Sierra Nevada
Walking in Andalucia
Walking in Menorca
Walking in the Cordillera
    Cantabrica
Walking on Gran Canaria
Walking on La Gomera and
    El Hierro
Walking on La Palma
Walking on Lanzarote and
    Fuerteventura
Walking on Tenerife
Walking on the Costa Blanca
The Camino Portugués
Walking in Portugal
Walking in the Algarve
Walking on Madeira

GREECE, CYPRUS AND MALTA

The High Mountains of Crete
Trekking in Greece
Walking and Trekking on Corfu
Walking in Cyprus
Walking on Malta

**INTERNATIONAL CHALLENGES,
COLLECTIONS AND ACTIVITIES**

Canyoning in the Alps
Europe's High Points
The Via Francigena
    Canterbury to Rome – Part 2

AFRICA

Climbing in the Moroccan
    Anti-Atlas
Mountaineering in the Moroccan
    High Atlas
The High Atlas
Trekking in the Atlas Mountains
Walks and Scrambles in the
    Moroccan Anti-Atlas
Kilimanjaro
Walking in the Drakensberg

TAJIKISTAN

Trekking in Tajikistan

JORDAN

Jordan – Walks, Treks, Caves,
    Climbs and Canyons
Treks and Climbs in Wadi Rum,
    Jordan

ASIA

Annapurna
Everest: A Trekker's Guide

Trekking in the Himalaya
Trekking in Bhutan
Trekking in Ladakh
The Mount Kailash Trek

NORTH AMERICA

British Columbia
The John Muir Trail
The Pacific Crest Trail

SOUTH AMERICA

Aconcagua and the Southern Andes
Hiking and Biking Peru's Inca Trails
Torres del Paine

TECHNIQUES

Fastpacking
Geocaching in the UK
Indoor Climbing
Lightweight Camping
Map and Compass
Outdoor Photography
Polar Exploration
Rock Climbing
Sport Climbing
The Mountain Hut Book

MINI GUIDES

Alpine Flowers
Avalanche!
Navigation
Pocket First Aid and Wilderness
    Medicine
Snow

MOUNTAIN LITERATURE

8000 metres
A Walk in the Clouds
Abode of the Gods
Fifty Years of Adventure
The Pennine Way – the Path,
    the People, the Journey
Unjustifiable Risk?

For full information on all our
guides, books and eBooks,
visit our website:
www.cicerone.co.uk

Walking – Trekking – Mountaineering – Climbing – Cycling

Over 40 years, Cicerone have built up an outstanding collection of over 300 guides, inspiring all sorts of amazing adventures.

 Every guide comes from extensive exploration and research by our expert authors, all with a passion for their subjects. They are frequently praised, endorsed and used by clubs, instructors and outdoor organisations.

All our titles can now be bought as **e-books**, **ePubs** and **Kindle** files and we also have an online magazine – **Cicerone Extra** – with features to help cyclists, climbers, walkers and trekkers choose their next adventure, at home or abroad.

Our website shows any **new information** we've had in since a book was published. Please do let us know if you find anything has changed, so that we can publish the latest details. On our **website** you'll also find great ideas and lots of detailed information about what's inside every guide and you can buy **individual routes** from many of them online.

It's easy to keep in touch with what's going on at Cicerone by getting our monthly **free e-newsletter**, which is full of offers, competitions, up-to-date information and topical articles. You can subscribe on our home page and also follow us on **Facebook** and **Twitter** or dip into our **blog**.

Cicerone – the very best guides for exploring the world.

CICERONE

Juniper House, Murley Moss, Oxenholme Road, Kendal, Cumbria LA9 7RL
Tel: 015395 62069 info@cicerone.co.uk
www.cicerone.co.uk